LONE OAK

LONE OAK

PHILLIP HARDY

TATE PUBLISHING
AND ENTERPRISES, LLC

Published by Tate Publishing & Enterprises, LLC
127 E. Trade Center Terrace | Mustang, Oklahoma 73064 USA
1.888.361.9473 | www.tatepublishing.com

Tate Publishing is committed to excellence in the publishing industry. The company reflects the philosophy established by the founders, based on Psalm 68:11,
"The Lord gave the word and great was the company of those who published it."

Book design copyright © 2015 by Tate Publishing, LLC. All rights reserved.
Cover design by Samson Lim
Interior design by Angelo Moralde

Published in the United States of America

ISBN: 978-1-62295-148-2
1. Fiction / Westerns
2. Fiction / Christian / Western
15.02.16

Dedicated to my beautiful bride, my children, and to the memory of Louis L'Amour. While I know I am nowhere near the author he was, my children all enjoyed *Lone Oak*. Characters throughout the book have some of the qualities of each of them. Each of them encouraged me throughout the process of writing *Lone Oak*. It is my sincere prayer that they all aspire to become closer to God and defenders of the defenseless. Even though it was written first, *Lone Oak* is the final book in the series that begins with *Vengeance is Mine*.

Introduction

*L*one Oak, by Phil Hardy, draws you in with action, adventure and a hero who is just an average guy doing what's right simply because it's the right thing to do.

James Harding rides into the small town of Lone Oak and straight into trouble. Dean Morrish and his pals have run roughshod over the townsfolk—but that is about to come to an end. The spoiled son of the largest rancher in the area has never run into someone quite like the average-looking, sarsaparilla-drinking man on the dusty buckskin horse. The mild-mannered stranger will allow himself to be belittled and pushed to a point. Then he pushes back, hard! But will the town of Lone Oak learn its lesson, or will James Harding finally meet his maker?

Prologue

Tiredly Jim dropped the reins of his horse. He had already taken in the youth and excessive bravado of his antagonist.

"Kid," he started, "I've told you this isn't your fight, but it looks like you're going to make it so. I don't want to draw on you, and you sure don't want to draw on me for two reasons. First, you aren't nearly fast enough, and second, if I have to kill you, where will you spend eternity?"

Clearly caught off guard, the young gunman wasn't sure what his next move should be. That question was answered when Jim's right-hand Colt seemed to just appear in his hand and spout flame. The pearl handle of The Kid's right-hand Colt disintegrated before he could even move his hand.

"I'm going to Aunt Mable's. Do you still have an objection to that?"

Chapter 1

Dust eddies swirled around the hooves of his buckskin gelding as he rode leisurely into town. He wasn't much different than any other drifting cowhand that rode through. About five eight and one hundred seventy pounds, he was what one would call average.

His clothes were travel-stained but in good condition. They, like him, were not flashy and could be bought at any mercantile that served cattlemen. That was with two exceptions.

His footwear was of excellent quality and was made specifically for him. That by itself was not noteworthy, but the style of footgear was. They were not a boot but rather a type of moccasin with a soft sole and lacing to the upper calf. The man who wore them would be just as at home on foot as in the saddle. That was something that you didn't see every day in the town of Lone Oak, at least not on the feet of someone who worked around cattle.

The other item that stood out was his gun belt. While the pistols themselves appeared to be single-action Colt revolvers, the gun rig was custom made. It rode on his hips as if permanently affixed in the perfect position for the swift withdrawal of either Colt. Well-oiled though dusty from travel, it showed considerable care without looking ominous.

The stranger rode to the hitching rail of the nearest place he could find that served food. Mickey's Pub and Grub looked like any of hundreds of other eateries where he had dined. It was hot, and he was hungry and thirsty, so Mickey's would do.

Swinging down from the buckskin, he tied the horse to hitching rail, stretched, and started for the door. It was approaching dinnertime, and several others were entering too.

One group consisted of three rowdy young men who seemed more interested in the pub than the grub part of Mickey's. All three were at least four inches taller than the rider and exuded a certain arrogance that rankled him. He had seen it before, and like many times before, he ignored it.

When he was seated, the waitress brought coffee and said with a tired but friendly smile, "We have beef steak, beef stew, or roast beef with all the trimmings. What would you like?"

When he looked up, the stranger could not help but return her smile. About five foot three, she had waves of red hair tied back to keep it from falling into her face or the plates of food she delivered. Freckles were splashed across the bridge of her nose, and her teeth were white and even behind her red lips. Long lashes surrounded her emerald green eyes. She was very pretty without being what one would call a classic beauty. Her smile seemed genuine instead of the forced ones that you sometimes saw. Her demeanor, even though she was tired, seemed friendly and demanded a smile in return.

Taking off his hat and running his fingers through his dusty brown hair, he ordered beef steak with all the trimmings. He caught the waitress off guard though when he ordered sarsaparilla to drink instead of beer.

"Sarsaparilla?" she almost shouted as she looked at his darkly tanned face to see if he was joking.

"Yes, ma'am," he replied. "As cold as you can get it, please."

The three rowdies had taken a seat nearby and overheard the order for sarsaparilla. Thinking it would be great fun to target the stranger for their vicious pleasure, they started in.

The largest and best dressed of the three sneered. "Sarsaparilla? Ain't that some kiddies' drink?"

"Why sure it is," one of his cronies piped in. "They ain't allowed to serve it to a full-growed man, don't you know? They say it'll turn you into a sissy if'n you drink it after you're all growed up."

The problem for them was that the stranger didn't take the bait.

While it riled him that the three were so obviously arrogant and disrespectful, he knew that taking up the fight would only end badly. He chose instead to ignore them.

When his meal and drink arrived, he bowed to pray, and the insults grew in intensity and vulgarity. About halfway through his steak, the largest of the three grabbed the waitress roughly by the arm and demanded, "Why're you waiting on that milksop honey when you could be servicing a real man?" When she tried to pull away, he refused to let her go and sneered at her lecherously.

A quiet voice reached the ears of everyone who had been watching. "Release the lady and have a sarsaparilla, *boy*, or somebody could become injured."

Momentary silence filled the room. Nobody in Lone Oak had ever talked to the three rowdies in such a fashion. It wasn't that they were all that well liked, but the ringleader's father owned the largest ranch in the area. That and the fact that the three were not opposed to beating a man silly just for fun made most people cautious around them.

After his initial shock wore off, the ringleader turned menacingly toward the speaker and shoved the waitress away. "Do you know who you're talking to, sissy boy?" he demanded. "I'll have you—"

Before he could finish, the stranger interrupted him. "I don't know you, but I know your type—the spoiled whelp of a rich daddy who thinks a foul mouth, money, and guns make him tough. You're a two-bit, snot-nosed brat who needs his pants pulled down and his backside paddled—something I would guess your daddy didn't do enough of. Did I miss anything?"

The voice was no longer as quiet as when the order to "release the lady" was given, but it was even, controlled, and laced with menace to any who cared to listen. To add to the insult, the stranger had not even bothered to rise from his chair or even look up to confront the trio. It was as if he were addressing some errant child.

He turned his attention back to his meal and shoved a bite of potato into his mouth just as the young man charged. Without much noticeable concern, the stranger shoved the chair on the opposite side of his table into the path of the charging bully. Unable to stop himself, the attacker's feet became tangled in the chair, and he crashed helplessly to the floor. Before he could gather his wits, the stranger was on him. Yanking the bigger man to his feet with deceptive ease, the stranger backhanded him with his right hand while propelling him backward toward his companions with his left. One, two, three ringing blows, and then a quick shove left him tangled with one of his cohorts.

The third member of the trio uttered several vulgarities and swung a wide, looping right at the stranger's head. Strong he might be, but fast enough he was not. The stranger easily ducked under the punch and threw an elbow into the armpit of his opponent, whose arm went immediately numb. Whether by design or accident, the stranger had struck a nerve, rendering the arm painfully useless for a short time. That was the least of the loudmouth's worries.

As he went under the punch, the stranger stepped past his antagonist so he was behind him. He spun and kicked the back of the young man's right knee, knocking it out of joint and rendering him useless in a hand-to-hand fight.

Meanwhile the instigator of the problem and his second companion had untangled themselves and were ready to head back into the fray. That proved to be a bad idea. Until then the stranger had held back, but now he was becoming angry. It was happening again. He stopped in a strange town, and some local wannabe-tough guy picked him for an easy target. It always ended badly for the local tough.

As the two charged toward him, he stepped in their direction and dropped his hands to the floor. Swiveling his legs in a sweeping motion toward the two, he knocked their legs from under them. The stranger was back on his feet before they hit the floor and delivered a powerful kick to the jaw of the town tough guy's friend. The crunch of breaking bone was audible throughout the room. The jaw was broken, and the tough was out cold. Fortunately for the ringleader, his head struck the edge of a table on the way to the floor, rendering him mercifully unconscious.

Even though he would be useless in hand-to-hand combat, the third member of the trio tried to redeem himself. He started to pull his pistol with his left hand. Before his pistol was halfway clear of leather, he found himself staring into the very large-looking muzzle of the stranger's own left-hand Colt. His draw halted, and he began to wonder if drinking sarsaparilla was really such a bad idea after all.

"What's your name, son?" the stranger asked calmly.

"D-Dwayne," was the stammered reply.

"Well, Dwayne, remember this the next time you decide to start in on a stranger." He waved his right hand at the groaning pair on the floor. "Now I would suggest that you take your friends and yourself to the nearest physician and let me finish my meal in peace."

With a quick flick of the wrist, the stranger holstered his Colt and returned to his table to finish his meal. Before he sat down though, he turned to Dwayne, who was helping his now semiconscious friends to their feet and said, "One other thing. Don't ever try to manhandle a lady in my presence again, or I will not be nearly as gentle."

Trying to salve his injured pride, the ringleader stopped at the door and hurled a threat back at the stranger. "You'd best be out of town before sunset!" He slammed the door and staggered toward the doctor's office with his badly limping and still groggy friends.

As the injured trio left for Dr. Halloran's office, talk began to well up once again. The stranger sat back down to resume his meal. He could hear the whispers. "He whipped them all with no more effort than it would take to swat a fly." Other similar comments were heard as well. All he could think was, *Not again, Lord. Not again.*

When the waitress returned to refill his coffee, she bent low and whispered, "Thank you for rescuing me. That Dean Morrish is a brute when he drinks, and the way he grabbed my arm hurt. One thing though—he will try to get even with you. Be careful, mister."

Looking into her face, he could see real concern. As she poured his coffee, he could also see the red marks left on her arm from the rough treatment. His father had taught him to treat women with respect and to never tolerate their mistreatment. Dean Morrish was very fortunate that he had not seen the bruises before the fight had started.

Smiling, the stranger responded to the waitress. "My name is James, ma'am. Please don't call me 'mister.' It makes me feel older than I already am. Call me Jim or James, please."

The waitress brightened and replied, "Well, James, my name is Elizabeth, and it is a pleasure to make your acquaintance."

With that, she was off waiting on other tables in the growing dinner crowd. He couldn't help but wonder about her. He didn't see a wedding ring, but that didn't necessarily mean anything. In this country luxuries, like jewelry, were sometimes neglected.

The dinner rush was on, so he didn't have the opportunity for further conversation. He paid four bits for his meal and left half that amount for a tip. He had enjoyed his meal and didn't mind leaving what most would consider an extravagant tip.

Having been directed to Aunt Mable's Boardinghouse by Joe, the owner of Mickey's, Jim set off in that direction leading his horse. It was a short walk, and he wanted to take his time and enjoy the evening air. Along the way, he saw Dr. Halloran's office and decided to check on the health of Dwayne and his other antagonists.

Wrapping the reins loosely around the hitching rail, he walked into the doctor's office. The office was clean, orderly, and well lit. Lining the walls was a library of medical and scientific books and equipment. The desk was set to the left side of the office to allow easy entry and to keep from blocking the two examining room doors in the back wall. Painted white to brighten the room, the office smelled of cleaning products and medicine. A set of stairs behind the desk led to the doctor's living quarters on the second floor.

From the door of one of the rooms emerged a tall, thin man in his mid-forties. His clean-shaven face and neatly trimmed, jet-black hair went well with the white lab coat and apron he was wearing. Both had a small smattering of blood on them. His black hair showed a few strands of gray in it, which only added to his air of competence and wisdom. Under his lab coat and apron he wore a starched white shirt and a black string tie. His gray trousers were neatly pressed, and his shoes were polished to a high luster.

"Dr. Halloran?" Jim asked.

"Yes, how can I help you?" was the reply. His voice was a deep, rich baritone with a Midwestern accent.

"There was an altercation at Mickey's, and I was stopping to check on the condition of some who were involved. I believe that they were coming here for treatment."

The doctor took a closer look at Jim, trying to decide why this man would be checking on his patients. He answered somewhat cautiously, "Dwayne and Jake are still here, but Dean headed back to the ranch already. I believe he was going to get The Kid to hunt down the ones that beat them. That's too bad. It will make more work for me and probably some for the undertaker as well. I hope the gang that did this has already left town."

A slight smile tugged at the corners of Jim's mouth as he thought of the story that the young rowdies must have told. Just then, the door to one of the examining rooms opened, and Dwayne limped out.

Stopping dead in his tracks, he swallowed hard and said sheepishly, "Mister, Dean headed back to the ranch to get The Kid. He plans to have him kill you for what you done. I'd get out of town before he gets back if I was you. The Kid's quick as a snake. He's killed men before."

Jim showed a tired smile and said, "Dwayne I didn't start that fuss, as you well know, and I plan to stay the night in town. I've ridden a long way, I'm tired, and I plan to sleep in a bed under a roof tonight. As far as I'm concerned, it's over. Now how are you and Jake doing? No permanent damage, I hope."

Dwayne's shocked expression was surpassed only by the bewildered look on Dr. Halloran's face. "We'll survive," replied Dwayne. "Jake's jaw is broke, and he'll be eating soup for a while. Doc was able to put my knee back in place. I'll be limping for a few days, but there's no permanent damage."

"Wait a minute," the doctor broke in, no longer able to contain his curiosity. "Do you mean that you are their 'gang' of attackers? One man?"

"Guilty as charged," Jim replied with a slight grin. "I'm just glad that there was no permanent damage."

"Well, I'll be…" the astonished medical practitioner breathed. "I'll be," he repeated as he looked at Dwayne, who seemed to tower over Jim but showed no inclination to resume hostilities.

After a few more inquiries, Jim started for the door. Dwayne stopped him with a question that had been nagging at him since leaving Mickey's.

"Hey, mister," he called. "Why didn't you shoot me? You could have and nobody would have questioned it, but you didn't. Why not?"

"Dwayne," Jim stated solemnly, "I didn't have to. God is the one that gave you life, not me. If I don't have to take it to protect others or myself, I'll leave it to him to do. I don't kill or injure someone just because I can. You get better and think about that while you're recovering. By the way, my name's Jim, not 'mister.'"

Without waiting for a reply, he stepped out the door. He sucked in a deep breath of night air, gathered his horse's reins, and resumed his walk to Aunt Mable's. It had been weeks since he had slept in a bed or had something besides his saddle or moccasins for a pillow, and he was looking forward to it.

Seventy or eighty yards short of Aunt Mable's front gate, Jim heard the hooves of racing horses. Stepping to the side of the road to allow them to pass, he noticed that one of the riders was Dean Morrish. In the fading light, a slight bruise on his forehead was the only evidence of the earlier fight.

The second man was not much more than a boy. He was maybe eighteen years old at the most with reddish-blond hair and a thin wisp of what some might generously call a mustache. He wore meticulous black clothing, and two pearl-handled Colts rode in tied-down black holsters. He was about Jim's height but thin and pale looking. This had to be the one that Dwayne and Dr. Halloran had called The Kid.

Dean spotted Jim just as they were about to pass by him. Yanking back cruelly on the reins, he brought his lathered mount to a halt before Jim. The Kid halted his palomino mare much more gently and studied the man at whom his employer glared.

"I thought I told you to get out of town," Dean snarled. "What're you still doing here?"

Trying hard to suppress his own anger, Jim looked at the black-dressed youngster while answering. "I was checking on Dwayne and Jake. They'll recover, although Jake will be eating soup for a while, and Dwayne will be limping for a few days. Now if you don't mind, I've ridden a long way, I'm tired, and I'm heading to Aunt Mable's for a hot bath, if she has them, and a long night's sleep in a comfortable bed."

Jim started on his way again. This time, the young gunman stopped him by swinging his horse into Jim's path. "I don't think the boss was done talking to you," he chirped in his still adolescent voice. "You can leave when and if he says you can!"

Losing his patience, Jim quickly took the two steps needed to reach the head of the young gunman's horse and struck the palomino a startling but harmless blow to the face with his hat. The frightened animal reared and began to lunge away from the surprise attack. Caught off guard, the gunman tumbled unceremoniously to the ground, and Jim whirled to face him.

"This isn't your fight," he growled. "I've been trying to relax and mind my own business after a long day in the saddle. Now leave me be!'

"As for you,"—he spun to face Dean—"*Mister* Morrish, you've been dragging your hired men into your trouble making since I walked into Mickey's. Two of your men are at Dr. Halloran's, and you're about to send this one"—he waved negligently at the black-dressed gunman who was rising from the dust—"to Boot Hill. For what? To harass a stranger who had done you no harm? I'm going to Aunt Mable's. Now stay out of my way!"

Jim turned toward his horse to gather the reins. As he did, the young would-be gunman spoke up. "You can't talk to Dean that way and get away with it, mister. Turn around and face me!"

Jim simply picked up the reins of his patiently waiting buckskin and started once again toward the boardinghouse. The youngster was beside himself with impotent rage. A small crowd had gathered, and this stranger was ignoring him. He had grown fond of being the center of attention and didn't like this situation one bit.

Hurling threats, he ran to cut Jim off one more time. "You can't walk away from me, mister," he fumed. "I'm going to cut you down!"

Tiredly, Jim dropped the reins of his horse. He had already taken in the youth and excessive bravado of his antagonist. "Kid," he started, "I've told you this isn't your fight, but it looks like you're going to make it so. I don't want to draw on you, and you sure don't want to draw on me for two reasons. First, you aren't nearly fast enough, and second, if I have to kill you, where will you spend eternity?"

Clearly caught off guard, the young gunman wasn't sure what his next move should be. That question was answered when Jim's right-hand Colt seemed to just appear in his hand and spout flame. The pearl handle of The Kid's right-hand Colt disintegrated before he could even move his hand.

"I'm going to Aunt Mable's. Do you still have an objection to that?"

Astonished, the Kid's eyes bugged out of his ashen face and his mouth hung open silently. He gulped once.

"I take it that means no." With that, Jim gathered the reins of his horse and stalked off to Aunt Mable's.

Chapter 2

Aunt Mable's was a large, two-story stone home at the edge of town with perhaps eight or ten rooms for guests plus a large kitchen, dining room, parlor, and library. Surrounded by well-kept flowerbeds, a white picket fence, and having one of the very few porch swings in town, the home could be called elegant by Western standards. Clean and neat as a pin, the house looked warm and inviting.

Aunt Mable herself answered the door in response to Jim's knock, and a broad smile deepened the wrinkles around her eyes and mouth. How old she was was anybody's guess. Her gray hair and seamed faced could place her anywhere from sixty to eighty years old, but her dark brown eyes still shined with merriment and just a touch of mischief.

Her eyes twinkled with delight as she ushered Jim into the house. "You get in here, young man," she ordered him gently. "I saw what you did out there, and it sure was something. I heard about what you did for Beth Ann down at

Mickey's too. You're sure enough welcome here. She is such a sweet girl, and that Dean had it coming to him."

She continued to cheerfully prattle on as she took his hand like an old friend and led him to a very nice upstairs room.

"Oh my," she exclaimed, "I didn't even ask if you wanted a room or not! You were wanting to stay the night, weren't you?"

"Yes, ma'am," was the simple reply. "You certainly have a beautiful place here. Do you get many boarders?"

"Oh, I manage to keep the rooms full most of the time. Since that Morrish crowd started their high and mighty shenanigans, it's been a little tougher. People don't want to stay around town much when they might get stomped just for smiling wrong. I was glad to hear what happened to Dean and his bunch, especially since it was in defense of Beth Ann."

"I don't want to seem ignorant, ma'am, but who is Beth Ann?" Jim inquired.

"Oh my, child, Beth Ann is Elizabeth. Elizabeth Angela Davis. I call her Beth Ann for short. She's one of my regular boarders and is such a delightful girl. I kind of watch over her as if she was my own. She helps with breakfast and the baking to help pay for her room."

"You have both men and women as tenants?"

"Certainly," replied Aunt Mable. "The ladies have their rooms downstairs, and the gentlemen stay upstairs. Everyone has breakfast together, but there are no ladies allowed upstairs, and no gentlemen are allowed in the ladies' area downstairs. Violate that rule and I'll toss you out on your ear!"

"No problem, ma'am," Jim responded. "By the way, is there somewhere that I can get a hot bath? I've been on the trail for a couple of weeks now, and I'm sure that I smell pretty ripe."

Aunt Mable assured him that she could accommodate him, and she made arrangements to have a youth that helped her haul a tub and hot water to his room.

While the water was heating, Jim stabled his horse in the barn behind the house and carried his possibles bag, rifle, and saddlebags back to his room. Once there, he got a cleaning kit from his saddlebags, stripped off his gun belt, and began to meticulously clean his Colts. In the middle of cleaning his second Colt, a knock came at his door. He answered it to find two young teenage boys carrying a large brass tub. Both boys stared in wide-eyed wonder at the man who had, in less than two hours, whipped the three biggest bullies in town and made The Kid look as slow as molasses in January.

After a couple of awkward minutes of silence, Jim smiled and spoke. "Can I help you?"

"Um, uh, well," began one of the boys who was shocked into speaking. "Aunt Mable said to fetch the tub for you. I brought Davie along to help."

"Well thank you, son," replied Jim. "Why don't you set it down over there to the side?"

The boys brought the tub into the room, all the time staring at Jim or the half-cleaned revolver on the bed. After bumping into several pieces of furniture, the boys set the tub down and started for the door.

At the door, the boy who had spoken earlier stopped as he remembered that they hadn't filled the tub yet. "I almost forgot," he stated. "Aunt Mable is heating water, and we'll bring it up when it's ready. Is that okay?"

"Of course," was Jim's reply. "Here's something for your trouble." He tossed a quarter to each of the boys. "There's another one for each of you when you bring the water up."

The boys' eyes bugged out of their heads as they alternated between gawking at each other, the coin, and the man in front of them. Fifty cents was more than an entire day's wage for either of them. Hauling the tub and water for this man who had the town buzzing was something that they would have done for free, and he was tipping them more than a whole day's pay.

"We'll get it up here as soon as it's hot, mister."

The boys hurried off, and Jim went back to cleaning his pistols. Once they were cleaned and properly lubricated, he reloaded them and wiped the holsters and ammunition from the belt with an oilcloth.

As he worked, he thought back to the time when he had the belt made. He had bought the Colts and practiced with them tirelessly for several hours every day. He found a leather smith that did exceptional work and gave him a description of what he wanted. The leather smith worked on the rig for several weeks, making it ride just right and hold the weapons perfectly. A better-made gun rig would be impossible to find.

Jim thought back to the advice given to him by the craftsman as well. *"I know why you want this rig,"* he said. *"Revenge is a powerful motivator, but it will eat your soul if you follow it too far. It's a dark master."*

Youth and rage had made him ignore the advice. How many had fallen because of it? He didn't want to think about it. He knew that he had broken free of his "dark master" only by the grace of God and the intervention of Preacher. What his real name was, nobody seemed to remember, but he had showed Jim the error of his ways in no uncertain terms. The final lesson had come at his death when he made a furious Jim promise not to seek revenge but to bring in his murders alive if possible. "God will see that they get their just reward," he said, and Jim reluctantly gave his word.

Three years had passed since then. He had kept his word, and all of those responsible for Preacher's death were brought to justice. One of them had talked to the local pastor the day before he was to be hanged. He asked Jim to forgive him for his part in killing his friend and mentor and said that he'd tell Preacher that Jim had kept his word. He seemed to know that he would see Preacher immediately after being hanged and was at peace with it. The next morning he faced the hangman with a calmness that showed on his face and was hung while singing "Amazing Grace."

Jim's reverie was interrupted by a knock at the door. Opening the door, he found his earlier visitors had returned bearing several buckets of hot water.

He smiled at the youth and let them in. Pouring the hot water into the tub, they filled it more than half full of the steaming liquid. Jim looked longingly at the tub. Digging the promised money from his pocket, he paid the young workers.

"Thanks, mister," was the response from the wide-eyed youth.

"I know Davie is his name," Jim said, "but what's yours, son?"

"I'm Tommy," was his awe-filled reply. "Do you need anything else?"

With a negative response, Jim sent the boys off merrily chattering to each other about his generosity and what they planned to do with their gains. It made Jim happy to be able to be so generous. It had not always been that way.

He turned his attention back to the tub. Locking the door, he got his bathing items out of his possibles bag. He always carried soap and his razor, and there were several washcloths and towels on the washstand near where the tub was. Placing his soap and razor on the washstand, he got a clean set of clothing out of his saddlebags and placed them neatly on his bed.

As was his habit, he placed his right-hand Colt on a chair close to the tub before undressing and climbing into the tub. He stripped off his shirt, revealing several scars on his strongly muscled torso. Most, but not all, were from his late teens just before he started down the path that nearly led him to become the very thing that he detested: mercilessness.

The scars were left by blows from whips and coiled ropes as well as hot coals and several bullet wounds. The small band of Indians that found him after his family had been slaughtered had given him a name that translated to "Can't Die." They believed that if he could survive what he had been through, he could not be killed by mortal man. For the next few years, he lived as if he believed it too.

He climbed into the tub facing the door and closed his eyes, letting the warm water soak away the dirt from his body and the memories from his mind. Sliding under the water, he soaked his hair and then scrubbed himself from top to bottom. With a couple of weeks' worth of dirt washed away, Jim was feeling relaxed and refreshed.

Exiting the tub, he dried himself, shaved, and donned clean clothes before heading downstairs to the parlor. He hoped to visit and gather some information before turning in for the night. He needed to find out where to get his laundry done and how to get the tub in his room emptied. He also wanted to know when breakfast was. He hated to miss breakfast when he was in town. That seemed like the only time that he could get bacon or ham and eggs. While bacon wasn't much of a problem on the trail, transporting eggs on horseback was difficult, at best.

When he entered the parlor, he nearly crashed into Elizabeth. She had returned from Mickey's sometime during his cleaning up and was coming out of the parlor as he was going in. Quickly recovering, he bowed slightly and said, "Good evening, Miss Davis. Please pardon me for not paying attention to where I was going."

"I'm afraid I wasn't looking where I was going either, Mister"—she paused—"I know your first name is James, but you never told me your last name."

The lamplight made her auburn hair fairly glow, and her blush nearly hid the freckles that were sprinkled generously across the bridge of her nose and cheeks. She too was embarrassed by their near collision.

"It's Harding, but I do wish that you would call me Jim or James. I feel awkward being called Mr. Harding."

"Then you must call me Elizabeth. I was going to get some coffee. Would you like some?"

"Of course," Jim replied.

When Elizabeth returned to the parlor, she found Jim in conversation with Aunt Mable and one of the other boarders, Dennis Sprague.

Dennis was a bespectacled young man with dark hair and eyes. He had an easy smile, and his plumpness added to his jovial appearance. His shopkeeper's shoes and jacket, along with his less-than-dark tan, left little doubt that he was a clerk at a local mercantile or perhaps a bank. It turned out to be the local bank where he had proved to be an honest and very competent teller.

Both men rose at Elizabeth's entry. She delivered Jim's coffee and was asked by Aunt Mable to join them. Since Aunt Mable insisted, she consented, and the group sat around talking about everything and nothing. Several other boarders stopped in the parlor to talk and relax. During this time, Jim asked about getting the tub in his room emptied, and Aunt Mable made arrangements to have it emptied before Jim got back to his room for the night.

While they talked, Jim learned a great deal of the local gossip and news as well as some of the local business owners' names and places of business. All of this information would be helpful if he stayed around for very long. He also learned about the families outside of town.

To the west of town, the Cabots had a small farm where they raised produce, and the Heinemanns had a herd of dairy cattle and dozens of laying hens. There was one farmer who had several broods of pigs and was reputed to produce some of the best ham and bacon for several counties. Several other homesteads were clustered to the west and north of town, where the ground seemed fertile, and to the east and south of town lay four cattle ranches. Only three of them were operating full time.

The largest of these was the Morrish ranch. The road running due east out of town ran right past the headquarters only three miles from town.

David Cochran owned the D/C to the south of the Morrish Swinging M, and west of him was the C&O of Clyde and Oliver Olson. They ran a small operation that provided most of the local beef. They kept a heftier breed of cattle called a white-faced with much more beef on the hoof than the usual longhorn, and they required far less room to roam. The problem was that they needed much more care and attention than their sturdy cousins from Texas.

The last ranch was a small well-situated ranch north and west of the Swinging M. Naturally bordered on the north by steep hills and covered with several small wood-lots, it was an ideal location. The well-watered meadows gave plenty of graze for livestock, and the woodlots pro-vided shelter during inclement weather. While this was by far the best range, it was the only ranch not being worked full time. That was a shock to Jim, but finding out that the owner of the S Bar S was none other than Elizabeth left him dumbfounded.

When he finally found his voice he said, only half in jest, "Beautiful, hardworking, friendly, and a landowner. I'm surprised you don't have beaus lined up for miles."

A sudden change came over Elizabeth. It wasn't anger, but she seemed to be hurt by Jim's comments and asked to be excused. As she left, Jim was again at a loss.

Aunt Mable told Jim that it was not his fault, and he couldn't possibly have known. She then went on to explain about the S Bar S and Elizabeth's ownership.

Several years before two young brothers, Samuel and Stephen Moss, had come to the area to make their mark. They arrived even before Thad Morrish, Dean's father, and had chosen the best range available for their enterprise. They filed for ownership of several square miles of land and the rights to thousands of acres. Things went well for some years, but when things got hard, Stephen sold out his share to Samuel and moved back east.

Not long after that, a young woman arrived in Lone Oak. With mounds of red hair and a smile that would melt an iceberg, Elizabeth was not shy of suitors. It was a couple of weeks before Samuel came to town, and when he did, it was for supplies, not to go courting. That soon changed. Elizabeth was working at the counter of the local mercantile when he walked in. He was young, handsome, and behaved as a gentleman should. Before long they were engaged to be married.

Two weeks before their wedding, he was found murdered on the roughest part of the S Bar S. In his will he left the ranch and all he had to his "beloved Elizabeth." It had been just over a year, and they had never found his killer. After telling the story, Aunt Mable went to comfort Elizabeth, and the men went to their rooms to turn in for the night.

Chapter 3

The next morning Jim was up before sunrise and spent the early morning in a deserted part of town doing his usual morning routine. It consisted of pushups, sit-ups, leg lifts, squats, stretches, another fifty or more pushups, a quick two-mile run, and then a series of wrestling, boxing, and hand-to-hand combat moves that went on for almost forty-five minutes. After that he stretched some more and washed up in the nearest rain barrel. He had done this for several of his twenty-nine years. Because of that, he might appear to be average, but his strength, endurance, speed, and dexterity exceeded that of a much larger man.

When he returned to Aunt Mable's, he was greeted by the smell of fresh coffee and frying bacon. Both smells made his mouth water. After shaving and changing his clothes, he returned to the dining room for breakfast, which proved to be delicious.

After the morning meal, Jim approached Elizabeth and apologized for his thoughtless comment from the night before. She reminded them both that he could not have known the facts and that his innocent comment would reopen wounds he knew nothing about. They talked briefly until she cleared the breakfast dishes and got ready for her workday a Mickey's. She worked there three days a week, leaving her the rest of the time to help at Aunt Mable's.

When the merchants, drummers, and everyone else had departed for their daily activity, Jim tried to find ways to help Aunt Mable around the boardinghouse. After splitting wood, cleaning the stable, and caring for his horse and the other two stabled there, he returned to the house to talk to her. He wanted to find out more about Lone Oak, and he still needed to find out where to get his laundry done.

The rest of the morning was spent in conversation with the boardinghouse owner. Jim got a pretty good lay of the land from her. Lone Oak was similar to most towns in southern Wyoming or northern Colorado. The name came from the fact that in the stand of aspen, birch, and poplar trees where the town was built stood a single, large oak tree. The town seemed to spring up around it, and the name seemed to fit. The lone oak still stood in the town square.

When lunchtime approached, Jim asked Aunt Mable if she would care to join him for the noon meal. Cheerfully accepting his offer, she laughed that a gentleman had not asked her to lunch for a long, long time.

"I sure hope that Beth Ann doesn't get jealous," she quipped as she took his arm, and the two strolled arm in arm toward Mickey's for lunch.

Aunt Mable seemed to be known and liked by everybody in town. She stopped to chat with several people along the way, making the five-minute walk take at least thirty minutes to accomplish. Jim didn't mind. He actually enjoyed being able to take a leisurely stroll through town. Aunt Mable seemed to be enjoying herself as well.

At Harper's Laundry, Aunt Mable led Jim inside and introduced him to the owners. "He's staying at my place, so make sure that he is well taken care of," she instructed them. "I'll have Tommy bring his things by later." The owners (Daniel and Lydia Harper) just smiled and agreed with her. They knew that her feigned sternness was just for show. They shook hands with Jim, and he and Aunt Mable continued their journey to Mickey's.

Since it was Saturday, the lunch crowd was light and spread out over a longer time than during the week. This gave Elizabeth a chance to visit with Jim and Aunt Mable. As long as all of his patrons were waited on, Joe didn't mind.

Talk came around to the ranch, and that gave Jim the opportunity to present an idea that he had.

"Elizabeth," he started, "Aunt Mable told me a little about your ranch and your situation. It sounds like the S Bar S could be a fine operation if it were worked properly. If you don't mind, I'd like to go to work for you in that regard. I'm at a point where I don't need the pay, but I do need to work. Would you be interested in hiring some no-account like me for room and board?"

Aunt Mable seemed to like the idea and chimed right in. "It's a wonderful idea. I'm a pretty fair judge of character, and I think he'll earn his keep. C'mon, honey. He just might help you keep the place. I know you love it, but you just don't know the cattle business. I'm betting Mr. Harding here does. Whitey's a good man, but he can't ride like he used to, and he's just one man."

Jim laughed. "Well I do know which end the hay goes in and which end it comes out."

Elizabeth looked from one to the other and tried to look upset. Instead she broke into laughter and asked, "Did you two have this planned before you got here? With my rescuer and my best friend conspiring together, how can I say no? One thing though, Mr. James Harding. I know how well you eat, so I expect a lot of work."

They all laughed, and the deal was sealed. Jim would be acting as ranch foreman. Since there were only two other punchers on the ranch, and one of them was only there when needed, that would not be a problem.

When the details were worked out, Jim asked if there was a church in town. Aunt Mable giggled. "Don't you think it's a little soon to be hunting up the preacher? You haven't proposed yet, and I haven't said yes yet either."

When the laughter died down, Jim was told that of course there was a church in town. Sunday morning at ten the doors would open, and the hymns would be sung.

"Would you escort me to services tomorrow morning?" he asked Elizabeth. "I'd be honored if you would."

"There's a church picnic afterward," Aunt Mable piped in. "It would do you some good to do something besides work."

"I don't know." Elizabeth began to protest. "I haven't been in more than six months, and you know how they liked to gossip, even if it was all lies."

"Gossip schmossip," Aunt Mable retorted. "You walk into that church on this man's arm on Sunday morning, and nobody would dare to gossip." Aunt Mable was as serious as Elizabeth had seen her in a long time. "Besides, if it's been over six months, it's high time you went. They don't say a thing when the soiled doves come in but a decent hardworking girl like you they don't want to darken their door? Shame on them! You go."

Elizabeth smiled sheepishly at the chastisement and said to Jim, "If you'll bring a buggy by at nine forty-five, I'll be ready."

After lunch, Jim got directions to the ranch. Armed with a letter of introduction from Elizabeth, he headed to the ranch headquarters.

During the ride out to the ranch, Jim paid close attention to the range conditions and to any cattle he saw on S Bar S range. The range conditions were excellent, but the number of cattle was not nearly what it should have been, and some of it was from the Swinging M. He made a mental note of the locations of the cattle and what brand they wore. The Swinging M cattle would have to be moved off the range, but why there were so few S Bar S cattle was something he needed to find out.

The one permanent employee of the ranch greeted Jim as he rode into the yard. He was an old-timer with plenty of snow on the mountain that most called Whitey. He was a couple of inches shorter than Jim, bowlegged, and had a large, bushy mustache stained with tobacco juice. Plenty of gray streaked the bushy eyebrows that sat above his steel gray eyes. Some might think him old and harmless, but only once.

As Jim introduced himself, he knew that he was being sized up. If Whitey thought he was a phony, he was sure that he would order him off the spread even with the letter.

Under the scrutiny of the cold, gray eyes, Jim did some sizing up of his own. All that he could see of this white-haired, bowlegged old puncher shaped up to his liking. He had been with the ranch from the beginning, demonstrating his loyalty, and he exuded a certain rawhide strength and toughness. He reminded Jim of Preacher in those ways.

"It 'pears Miss Elizabeth sets some store by you, boy. Why don't you climb down and come on in. I'll give you the two-cent tour and the rundown of the situation."

Whitey led the way into the kitchen and poured them both a cup of strong black coffee. After adding sugar to his, he pulled out a chair and straddled it, facing Jim across the table.

"I looked over what I could on the way out," Jim said. "The range is in great shape, but I only saw a few head of S Bar S cattle. The range should easily support ten times what I saw. What gives?"

"We had about three or four times as many cattle and a large remuda of horses before Sam got killed. We've been losing stock regular since then. I can't be everywhere, and the rustlers know it. I've been concentrating on bringing what I can find in closer to headquarters and holding the horses. Several of the creeks run all summer, so the range is good year round. I've managed to keep the remuda from being raided for the most part, but we have lost a few."

The remainder of the afternoon was spent going over range conditions, stock conditions, and a host of other items pertaining to the ranch and its operation. Both men seemed to be satisfied with their earlier assessments of each other.

Shortly before sundown, the men made a meal of beef and beans. Jim asked about a buggy and what the best route to town would be. Whitey figured that it would take about two hours, taking your time, to get to town driving a buggy. There was a good buggy horse in the barn that needed the exercise.

After dinner, the men checked the buggy and harness over to make sure that they were in good shape for the morning.

Chapter 4

Sunday morning dawned bright and sunny with just enough of a nip in the air to prove that it was still spring. Jim had already been up and had gone through an abbreviated version of his exercise routine. When Whitey awoke, he was only half surprised to see Jim already up, shaved, and dressed. To his way of thinking, the foreman should be up first but not by much. Besides that, he had gotten lazy lately and had begun to sleep in until almost six o'clock.

When he smelled the coffee, he realized that the new foreman had been up for longer than he had previously thought. He would have been very surprised if he knew that it had been well over an hour since Jim had climbed silently out of bed and started his morning routine.

Seeing Whitey open his eyes and stretch, Jim greeted him, "Good morning, sunshine. Glad to see you finally getting up and about." Jim was smiling, and Whitey knew that he was just haranguing him.

"I knowed you was up," he said. "I just wanted to make sure you had my coffee ready before I climbed out of bed."

Pouring two mugs of steaming black liquid, Jim asked about a skillet to make breakfast.

"Oh no, you don't! I'll be doggoned if I'll have the ranch foreman acting as cook," Whitey fumed. "You can make coffee if you want, but I'm not going to have you wet nurse me by cooking my breakfast too. Next thing you'll be trying to make my bed for me or saddle my horse. No, sir. I'll cook breakfast!"

That was that. Whitey dug out all of the supplies he needed and started breakfast. Eggs, hotcakes with maple syrup, and bacon were the fare for the morning, and Whitey proved to be quite adept as a cook. Apparently he had learned more than cow punching over the years.

As they were hitching the buggy, Jim asked, "Whitey, why don't you take the day off and come on into town with me? You've been out here seven days a week by yourself for a while. You need a break. Besides, I have a feeling, from what Aunt Mable said, that this could be a very interesting church service."

Whitey laughed. "I ain't darkened the church doors in quite a spell. I reckon I didn't like being compared to a dumb sheep. To be honest with you, the preaching got pretty boring with the 'thee's' and 'thou's,' and they didn't seem too fond of us with cow smell on our boots. Of course, if your going to church is like you riding into town for the first time, count me in."

Both men chuckled, and Jim knew that the "prairie telegraph" was working just fine. Somebody had seen what happened in town on his arrival, and now half of the county probably knew. When he asked Whitey what he had heard, he told him that their part-time puncher had been in Mickey's when the fight took place.

"He told me it was the most lopsided fight that he had ever seen. Said it took you less time to whip Dean, Jake, and Dwayne than it usually takes to brand a calf."

Chapter 5

The brilliant pinks and purples had barely been washed from the sky by the bright sunshine when the two headed for town. Wearing his Sunday suit, Jim was perched on the seat of the buggy, ready for the ride to town, when Whitey reemerged from the bunkhouse. He was wearing a clean white shirt, black string tie with a turquoise clip, black Levis, highly polished boots, and his best Stetson. He had saddled his horse earlier, so he swung astride, looking both uncomfortable at being dressed up and pleased with himself for having the clothes just in case. With Whitey in the lead, they started for Lone Oak.

Arriving at Aunt Mable's with plenty of time to spare, the men were led into the dining room to have coffee while they waited. Aunt Mable made her coffee strong and kept a pot on the stove almost twenty-four hours per day. While Jim sipped his just the way it came out of the pot, Whitey added several spoons of sugar to his, tasted it, then added several more. Aunt Mable noticed this and told him, "You should add some more, you old coot, if you really think it will sweeten you up." Thus began a friendly bickering between the two of them that kept up until exactly nine forty-five when Elizabeth entered the room.

Dressed in a blue cotton dress that contrasted well with her red hair and fair complexion, she blushed deeply when she noticed Jim staring her way. The dress accentuated her feminine lines without being immodest. A small, blue bonnet was perched jauntily atop mounds of auburn curls. In a word, she looked stunning.

Jim rose quickly to his feet but had trouble finding his voice.

Aunt Mable noticed this and laughed merrily. She poked Whitey, who also grinned at his young and otherwise competent foreman.

"Well quit your gawking, shut your mouth, and tell her how pretty she is, you dope." Aunt Mable giggled. "Then you take her by the arm and walk her to the buggy. I can write out the instructions if you want me to." Unable to contain themselves both oldsters broke into fits of laughter.

Blushing deep enough for it to show through his dark tan, Jim turned to scowl at his elders before he began to speak. His natural coordination seemed to be lost as he nearly dropped his coffee cup, setting it on the table, and tangled his feet as he stepped away from his chair. This drew even more snickers from the two eldest occupants of the room.

Regaining his breath and his composure, Jim bowed gallantly to Elizabeth and said in a most formal fashion, "Miss Davis, you look more lovely this morning than a desert rose in the early morning sunshine. Would you do me the honor of allowing me to escort you to this morning's service?"

"It would be my pleasure, Mr. Harding," she replied. With that, she took Jim's offered arm, and they started for the door. As they walked past Aunt Mable, Elizabeth couldn't resist the impish impulse to stick out her tongue at her best friend, and the two ladies had their own quiet chuckle.

"Well, Miss Mable, we cannot allow such tender youngsters to travel without a proper chaperone. Will you allow me to escort you to the same destination as our young charges?"

"Why, Whitey McKay, I don't believe I have ever heard you be so formal about anything in all my life. I suppose I will let you tag along after all," she responded. "Besides, if I leave you here to drink coffee, I won't have any sugar left by the time I get back."

They both laughed like the old friends that they were and, locked arm in arm, followed the younger couple to the buggy. Whitey helped Aunt Mable to the seat beside Elizabeth and, mounting his horse, he rode alongside the buggy toward the church a little west of town. He had a feeling that even if the services weren't interesting, the picnic afterward was sure to prove entertaining.

There were several buggies and wagons already pulled up in the meadow in front of the church when the S Bar S entourage arrived. Halting the buggy near a large tree so that the horse would have shade, Jim sprang to the ground and lifted Elizabeth effortlessly to the grass beside him. As Whitey dismounted and tied his horse in the shade, Jim circled the buggy and lifted Aunt Mable from the buggy as well.

Several heads turned to watch the small group start for the open church door. Aunt Mable greeted most of the families, but it was easy to tell that several were cool toward

Elizabeth. She could serve them food at Mickey's, but their demeanor clearly indicated that she was not entirely welcome at their church. Even the pastor's greeting was somewhat reserved.

When Elizabeth started to protest and tried to retreat to the buggy, Jim held tightly to her arm and smiled at her reassuringly. "They'll have to accept the fact that this is God's house, not their exclusive club. If they don't like it, they can take it up with Him or me, if He's busy." She clung tighter to his arm and smiled in return.

"Thank you," was all she said, but it was enough.

Arm in arm they walked to a seat near the front of the church sanctuary. The pew was empty when they sat down, and except for Aunt Mable, Dennis Sprague, and a pretty little brunette named Janie, it remained that way. Janie snuggled close to Dennis, who put his arm protectively around her shoulder. Whitey had elected to stand in the back of the church to watch what transpired from there.

As the rest of the congregation filed in and found their seats, they greeted each other but to a person neglected to greet Jim, Elizabeth, or even Aunt Mable. This type of rudeness in God's house raised Jim's hackles. If it continued, he was going to have to read to them from the Good Book, possibly the part about "smiting them hip and thigh" and definitely the part about "welcoming strangers."

When the preacher started leading them in singing the hymns, Jim was glad that the Scriptures said to "make a joyful noise," not a beautiful one, because there was more than one parishioner that could have used a bushel basket and still not been able to carry a tune. He considered his own gravelly baritone voice to be in that category. One welcome exception to that was the beautiful soprano voice of the young woman who stood beside him as they lifted their voices in reverential song.

Partway through "A Mighty Fortress Is Our God," the singing was interrupted by the clatter of horses' hooves and the creak of saddle leather. During the confused cessation of singing, a small cavalcade of cowpunchers walked through the open door of the church.

They were led by an older, tougher version of Dean Morrish. Though shorter and broader than his son, the family resemblance was obvious. Jim had no doubt that this was the "Old Bull," Thaddeus Morrish.

"Sorry about the interruption, Parson," boomed Thad. The deep base was exactly what one would expect when the powerful barrel chest of the man backed it. As sure of himself as he was, he knew that it was best to offer an apology for entering late and in such a noisy fashion. "We had some problems getting started this morning, but I told the boys if they wanted to go to the picnic, they had to listen to the preachin' first."

"That is quite all right, Mr. Morrish," was the timid reply from the preacher. "Please find a seat, and we'll get started again. And thank you for joining us this morning."

There was no room for the whole group to sit together, even though several parishioners moved to make room for them. Dwayne saw Jim and Elizabeth and limped forward to ask if he could join them. He was the only one of the Morrish hands that didn't sit as part of the crew.

"Of course you can," Jim quickly said. "I'm glad to see you out and about."

The singing started again, and the services proceeded from where they had left off. Jim was getting an idea about the preacher that was not altogether flattering. His timid response to the Morrish crew interrupting and the obvious subservient tone he used when addressing Mr. Morrish left little doubt in Jim's mind that he jumped when Thad said, "Frog."

The rest of the service was uneventful, but storm clouds were brewing. During the picnic, they would let loose.

Chapter 6

As church let out and the picnic began, Jim found a spot in the shade for himself and the two ladies whom he had escorted. Food and punch were served, and everyone seemed to be having a good time. Whitey had drifted off to talk to some of the punchers he knew from the D/C and C&O ranches. While most of the Swinging M congregated together, Dwayne stood off to the side near the food table and flirted with some of the young ladies in attendance, including one very pretty blonde.

The arrival of four drifters drew little attention at first since strangers were always welcome. Their leader was a huge brute of a man named Connors. His attitude drew attention shortly after their arrival for he was belligerent and coarse with everyone. It was obvious that he was spoiling for a fight.

A quiet suggestion from Dean gave him a target for his brutality. James Harding was a stranger and had humiliated Dean twice. Connors would exact revenge for Dean and take great pleasure in it. If he failed, they were both strangers anyway.

Starting with the insults aimed at Jim, Connors tried to goad him into a fight. "Ain't you that sarsaparilla-drinking sissy boy that just come to town?" taunted the giant. "What's the matter? Can't you handle a real man's drink?"

"If you're addressing me," Jim replied calmly, "my name is James, not 'sissy boy,' but I do like sarsaparilla. My friends call me Jim, but you may call me Mr. Harding. Try to remember that, if you can, and the fact that this is a church picnic and hardly the place for a fight. That is what you're trying to start, isn't it?" By going right to the heart of Connor's intention, Jim let everyone know that he was not the one starting the fight, but he would not be bullied either.

Whitey saw what was taking place and left the group he was standing with to take a hand if he was needed. Dwayne had also noticed what was taking place. He had also noticed the quick conversation between Dean and the truculent stranger.

Ever since the incident at Mickey's, he had been doing a lot of soul searching. He usually just went along with whatever Dean said and followed where he led. When he reflected on his life, he knew he had to make some changes. He too moved to where he could take a hand if needed.

"Are you calling me stupid?" Connors querulously asked.

"I wouldn't presume to know your intelligence or lack thereof. I merely suggested that you try to remember my name and that this is a church picnic. If you have trouble remembering that, well then I guess you weren't your teacher's brightest pupil." Jim knew that things were leading to a fight, and he knew that he would be unable to avoid it, so why try.

As the brutish Connors came toward him, Jim rose to his feet and moved away from Aunt Mable and Elizabeth to meet the giant. He did not want the fight close to them where they might be accidentally injured. Before beginning to eat lunch, he had removed his jacket so all he had to do was stand and meet his adversary.

"I'm gonna break you to pieces, Sarsaparilla," Connors boasted with a wicked grin.

Jim simply hit him. It was a well-thrown punch backed by hard muscles, and it landed squarely on the brute's jaw. It made him stop in his tracks and shake his head. Then he came on a bit more cautiously. Connors was strong and could take a punch. If he proved to be a competent fighter and not just tough, Jim was going to be in for a rough time.

Connors moved toward Jim smiling cruelly. His crooked yellow teeth showed between his thin lips as he balled his fists and moved in. Size and brute strength had won his fights or intimidated others into surrender, so he was unprepared for what happened next. Instead of being fearful and backing away, Jim stepped forward and pulped the bigger man's lips with a quick, powerful right and followed with a solid left to the wind. The power of the blows was more than Connors expected, and he stopped long enough to spit out blood and broken teeth.

"I'll kill you for that," Connors promised. "I'll do it with my bare hands right in front of your lady friend." As he finished speaking, he threw a roundhouse punch that would have flattened a bull. For that to happen, though, it had to connect. By the time the punch arrived where Jim had been, he was no longer there.

Preacher had taught Jim: "In a fight, you need to use your head for something besides blocking punches." Over the years, he had found that to be very sound advice.

Ducking the punch, Jim threw a hard left to the ribs and aimed a right at the soft spot just under the breastbone. What he hit was a stomach that felt like an oak plank. The fight was on.

Deftly blocking or deflecting most of the punches with his arms or shoulders, Jim continued to inflict punishment on the bigger man. A hard left swelled the brute's right eye, and a right made his ears ring before he managed to land powerful right to Jim's chest, sprawling him to the ground. Sensing what he thought was victory, Connors raced forward to put the boots to this upstart that had been besting him so far.

Jim was wearing his boots today instead of his moccasins. As Connors rushed in, he found himself running into those hard soles. The left boot caught Connors in the upper thigh, and the right boot struck him squarely in the belly button. Air whooshed out of his lungs as he reeled backward. Jim quickly sprang back to his feet.

Connors came in again. Suddenly, he leaped forward and managed to catch Jim in a bear hug. Squeezing tightly, he whispered to Jim, "I'm gonna break your back and leave you a cripple." If Jim couldn't break the hold that was exactly what would happen.

Bringing his forehead down onto the bridge of Connors's nose with all his strength, Jim smashed it like a ripe melon. The second time he did it, Connors howled and let go. Springing clear, Jim swiftly followed up his advantage. He smashed hammer-like blows to Connors's face and body.

The giant swayed like a huge pine in a strong wind before toppling to the ground.

Seeing their leader beaten, the remaining drifters started to move forward only to be stopped by a smiling, white-haired puncher with a drawn six-gun. "You boys wasn't thinkin' of bothering the S Bar S foreman, now was you? You see, I'm kinda fond of him, and I reckon your partner got what he was asking for. Just settle down now, and maybe my shaky, old fingers won't accidental-like pull the trigger."

All of them knew that if Whitey pulled the trigger, it wouldn't be accidental-like, and somebody was bound to get a lethal dose of lead poisoning. Besides, Connors was a big boy, and he did pick the fight.

Jim wearily walked back toward Elizabeth and Aunt Mable. Connors had been tough, and the punches that had gotten through had taken their toll. His shirt was torn, and he knew that he would be carrying several new bruises by morning.

Elizabeth came toward him but stopped suddenly and screamed. A shot rang out, and Jim spun to see Connors topple to the ground a second time. This time he would not be getting up again. Clutched in his right hand was his unfired Hopkins revolver.

"He was going to shoot you in the back, Jim. I couldn't let him do it." Dwayne was speaking and holding a still smoking pistol in his hand.

"I sure do appreciate that," Jim said, thankful for Dwayne's intervention. "I'm not even heeled today."

Several people rushed forward once they knew that it was safe. Among them were Dean and Thad Morrish. Seeing the chance to perhaps run the man who had embarrassed his son and therefore the Swinging M out of town, Thad's voice boomed out over the rest.

"Not even in town a week and he's been in two fistfights, a gunfight, and now this man is dead. What kind of a man is this?" he asked, pointing at Jim. "A trouble hunter, I'd say. And he shows up at our church picnic like he's some kind of Christian. I hardly think he's the kind we need around here."

Jim was growing tired of being a target just because he was new in town. He'd seen people in this town kowtow to this man and his ranch crew just because he owned the largest ranch in the area. They would be surprised if they knew about the Lazy H he owned in Southwest Montana.

The mining portion of it alone provided him with a very substantial income. The ranch portion covered thousands of acres and provided beef for the army and the reservations in the area. He was a very wealthy man but had not yet settled down to the life of being a ranch and mine owner. He knew that he would have to someday but not yet. Something was still missing for that to happen.

"Don't start, Mr. Morrish," Jim responded. "I tried to avoid those confrontations but was forced into each of them. Your own son started the first two. Each time I was attacked and acted to defend others or myself. I don't hunt trouble, but I'm ready if it comes. Even Jesus said if you don't have a sword, sell something and buy one. He believed in defending yourself and others. He's also the one that made a scourge and drove the moneychangers from the temple. I guess He was a trouble hunter too.

"He did say something about welcoming strangers though, and in the book of James, He said, 'To him that knoweth to do good and doeth it not, to him it is sin.' I sure haven't felt welcomed, and when Miss Davis was being manhandled, nobody here did what was good and right, which would have been to defend her. On top of that, I thought that this was God's house, not yours."

Dwayne spoke up. "He's right, Mr. Morrish. Dean, Jake, and me started that fuss at Mickey's. It wasn't until Dean grabbed Miss Davis that Jim did anything. We was getting pretty rude, but he just ignored us. I even tried to drag iron at the end of the fight. He could have killed me, and nobody'd of said nothing, but he didn't. He had me dead to rights, and he just told me to help get Dean and Jake to Doc's and let him finish his meal in peace. He even come by to see if we was all right."

"Are you taking his side?" Thad asked incredulously. "You're siding against me? You're fired! Be off the ranch before supper."

"I'm sorry you feel that way, Mr. Morrish, but I'm just being honest. I'll draw my time and be cleared out before supper."

"You'll draw nothing! I don't pay people to be disloyal," Thad boomed. He was not used to not getting his way.

Dwayne turned red in the face as his anger came to the surface. "I've got a month's wages coming!"

"You've got nothing coming! Be off the ranch by supper."

Dwayne started to protest. The rest of the Swinging M crew had gathered, and he knew it was no use, but he was going to try. The crew might disagree with Thad, but they rode for the brand.

Jim's voice cut through the tense silence. He had no desire for there to be any more shooting if it could be avoided. "Dwayne, you're hired. Supper will be a little late tonight, but you're on the payroll as of now. We need some more punchers on the S Bar S, and I prefer honest ones. I think you'll fit the bill. I'll even make good on the wages that Mr. Morrish owes. I have to warn you though that there is plenty of work to do."

"Yes, sir. I'll be there with bells on." Dwayne was glad to have a way out without being in a fight he knew he would lose. Relaxing visibly, he grinned and joined Jim and Whitey. In a lower voice he said, "I reckon you saved me from gettin' dead again. I owe you one."

"No, you don't," Jim replied. "I think you're a good hand. You were just on the wrong ranch. Besides that, you'll earn your keep."

The picnic broke up, and the undertaker collected Connors's body for burial.

Chapter 7

Elizabeth was noticeably shaken on the ride back to Aunt Mable's. Jim had been through and witnessed many gun battles, but it was a new and unsettling experience for Elizabeth. Unsure exactly what to do, he placed a reassuring arm around her shoulders. Turning her face against his body, she sobbed softly.

Aunt Mable watched the interaction and smiled. Elizabeth deserved a man that would care for her and make her feel safe. She was pretty sure that Jim would do just that. She also had a feeling that Jim had a need to be needed. He was definitely needed at the S Bar S and maybe, just maybe, by Elizabeth as well.

As he helped Elizabeth from the buggy, she dabbed at her tears and said, "I'm sorry. I just…I just…" Her voice trailed off, and she began to weep again. Jim pulled her gently to him and let her tears soak his shirt.

"I know," he whispered. "I am sorry you had to see such violence, but it will be all right." She seemed to take some comfort from Jim's calm confidence.

Suddenly she remembered the hiring of Dwayne. "Jim, you hired a new man, but I don't know how long or if I can even afford to pay him. What are you going to do if I can't afford it?"

"You let me worry about that when the time comes. I've got a feeling that your ranch will be profitable again very soon. Whitey is a worker and loyal, and I think Dwayne is a good man. I can always ask him if he wants the same pay the foreman gets." Remembering their agreement, they both chuckled slightly, and the terrible image of Connors lining his gun on Jim's back faded to the back of her mind.

"You keep holding her like that, and we're going to have to go get the preacher," Aunt Mable chided mildly.

Realizing that he was still holding Elizabeth gently in his arms, Jim released her and stepped back quickly. Elizabeth just smiled shyly at him and lowered her eyes. It had felt so natural to Jim to hold her that he didn't realize he hadn't let go until Aunt Mable spoke up.

After leaving the ladies at the boardinghouse, Jim sent Whitey to locate their part-time puncher and headed back to the ranch. Monday morning would see the entire crew hard at work. Jim wanted an accurate count of cattle and horses as well as an assessment of their condition and range conditions. He also wanted any Swinging M cattle moved off the range and back onto their home range as soon as possible.

Jim had the buggy put away and the black gelding half curried by the time that Whitey arrived with another puncher in tow. In his mid-twenties, with brown, curly hair, the new arrival looked slick and confident. He was dressed a bit too well for a part-time puncher, but he might have other income.

"Whitey, you don't mind doing the cooking, do you? You do a bang-up job of it, and we can't afford a full-time cook."

"Sure thing, boss. This here is Tyler. I told him it was time to earn some pay rather than spend it."

"Grab a bunk and settle in. Dwayne should be here shortly. Whitey, if you could get dinner going, we can talk about what we will be doing for the next few weeks while we eat. I plan to start early tomorrow, so I don't want to be up all night. We'll go over some of my rules while we're at it. There aren't many, but they don't bend."

Dwayne arrived a short time later with his personal belongings and mount. He no more than got his gear into the bunkhouse than Whitey gave a holler. "Food's on. Come and get it before I throw it to the hogs!"

The men obediently trooped to the table after washing in a basin just outside the door and sat down. Beefsteak, beans, and sourdough biscuits with honey adorned large plates on the table. The tempting smell filled the room as the food began to be passed around the table.

"Before you fellers dig in, one of my rules is if I'm at the table, I thank God for the food before we eat."

Tyler laughed. "If Whitey's cooking, you'd better thank God it doesn't kill us."

"If you think you can do better, you cook," was Whitey's hot retort.

"If you two don't mind, I'll continue. No booze, no fighting with each other, and I expect a full day's work for a full day's pay, and one last rule. If I catch you stealing from here or anywhere else, I'll fire you and set you afoot no matter where it is, when it is, or what it is."

"No booze?" It was almost a whine from Tyler. "That's almost inhuman."

"No booze! I've seen plenty of good men make foolish mistakes and get themselves or others killed while drinking. While working or on this range, that rule stands. If you can't handle it, the door is over there." Jim indicated the open front door of the bunkhouse. When Tyler didn't move, Jim continued. "Are there any other questions or comments?" He paused. "If not, let's get started."

Jim's prayer was quick and simple. The men quickly moved the food from their plates to their stomachs. While the meal was being devoured, Jim gave an outline of what needed to happen. The location of S Bar S cattle and horses needed to be found and an accurate count made. Cattle from other ranches needed to be hazed back to their home range, and any possible routes for rustling had to be located and checked for activity. That and the regular day-to-day ranch work had to be done.

The men would work in pairs and move cattle from rough country, where they might be stolen without notice, to more open range where they could be better kept track of. For the first day or two, Jim would work with Whitey to get better acquainted with the lay of the land. Whitey knew the range better than either of the other hands. After that, the men would take turns working with the foreman. When Swinging M cattle were being hazed back to their home range, Jim was always to be present.

"Any questions?" he asked after outlining his plans. "If not, enjoy your night because we'll be starting early tomorrow. Anybody still snoring when the sun comes up might as well pack up. We've got too much work to do to be sleeping in."

The first false predawn light was barely touching the eastern horizon when Jim finished his morning workout and had coffee ready. Whitey had breakfast going when the other two punchers stomped their feet into their boots and headed for the backhouse.

Dwayne greeted the day with a renewed energy. He felt like a huge weight had been taken off of his shoulders now that he was no longer working for Thad Morrish and the Swinging M. He hadn't realized how much he missed the early morning and just being a cowpuncher.

Tyler, on the other hand, was up and around, but he didn't look too happy about it. He gave the impression that he would just as soon not start work until the sun was much closer to its zenith. There was a definite difference between the joking, young puncher from the night before and the rather surly man this morning.

By the time Dwayne and Tyler returned from their morning constitutional, Whitey had breakfast on the table. Eggs, biscuits, ham, and potatoes filled the plates, ready for consumption. After the men sat down and Jim asked the blessing, the only sound that was heard was the sound of forks scraping plates and men chewing. In a matter of minutes, the plates were empty. The men leaned back contentedly and began to drink mugs of thick, steaming coffee before they started their work for the day.

"I take back what I said about your cooking." Tyler was beginning to brighten somewhat. "That breakfast was almost as good as the time I had to eat my saddle over in Utah."

Whitey looked like he was going to throw a skillet at Tyler, But Tyler continued earnestly. "That sure was a good saddle." Tyler, Jim, and Dwayne all laughed enthusiastically.

"You keep laughing, and I'll serve you all pack saddle soup for dinner!" The men laughed all the harder, and

Whitey muttered something about "ungrateful, young no-accounts." His reaction only brought more snickers, but when the laughter died down, all of the men gave Whitey compliments on his cooking. It never paid to anger the cook *too* much.

The men sucked down the last of their coffee and started for the corral. Selecting their mounts in the predawn chill, the men were saddled and headed out of the ranch yard just as the sun peeked above the horizon.

Chapter 8

The next several days were a whirlwind of work as the men cleared waterholes, pushed cattle from the rough breaks to more open range, and scouted the range for any sign of rustlers. The men worked from before sunup to well after full dark.

At the end of the second week, Whitey shot a big tom cougar as it was feeding on a yearling heifer that it had just killed. Jim raced to the scene with his gun drawn only to find Whitey calmly skinning the big tom. His shot had caught the cougar behind the left ear and killed it instantly.

The smell of blood and cougar made Jim's horse fidgety, and it took him a couple of minutes to bring it under control. The buckskin had been trained to remain calm during gunfire, but his young life had been spent in the wild, and his instinctive fear of cougars was deeply ingrained.

"They say there's more than one way to skin a cat, but I prefer 'em dead before I start. You done playing bronc-cobuster, or you gonna keep it up so's you don't have to help with the skinning?" Whitey seemed quite pleased with himself. "I knew this old puma was up here, but this is the first shot I had at him. This ain't the first of our stock he's killed either."

Jim dismounted from his now calm horse. The cat was easily one hundred and seventy pounds and was at least eight feet from nose to tail. He looked in awe at the huge cat. "He's no kitten. That's for sure. Of course, back home in Montana we keep them just about that size around the house for killing mice."

"They'd have to be some mighty big mice to feed this kitty." The men quickly finished skinning the cougar. When the task was finished, Whitey removed several choice cuts of meat from the carcass and wrapped them in the fresh hide. "He's been feeding on Miss Elizabeth's beef for a while. I reckon it's fair that he feeds us tonight. You ever ate cat before?"

"I spent two years with the Cheyenne. It has been a few years, but that's one dish I do miss. I was hoping you knew how to cook it and weren't going to let it go to waste."

Whitey grinned as he tied the hide-wrapped bundle of meat behind the saddle of his mount.

"Why don't you head in early and get started. I'll go find the others and give them a hand until time to come in." Without waiting for a reply, Jim mounted and headed off in the direction that Dwayne and Tyler were supposed to be working.

Forty-five minutes of riding brought Jim to the area where Dwayne and Tyler should have been. Hearing the sound of cattle and catching the scent of dust, Jim sped his horse up to a gentle lope. The scene that he came upon was not what he had expected.

Dwayne was confronting three armed men, and Tyler was nowhere in sight. Jim approached cautiously and stopped beside Dwayne.

"What gives?" he demanded. Jim had noticed that more than two hundred head of S Bar S cattle were gathered for travel, but they seemed to be pointed in the wrong direction. He also noticed that the three strangers were not only armed but had their weapons drawn and pointed at Dwayne. At least one of them swung to cover him as he approached. That was an express gun carried by the apparent leader of the group. The threat was unmistakable, but Jim didn't flinch. One more time he demanded, "I asked, what gives?"

"I come up on these three pushing S Bar S cattle north rather than south. They got the drop on me just as you rode up." Dwayne was mad clean through, but he had been caught flatfooted. He hoped that Tyler would show and take a hand, but he didn't let on that there was another S Bar S hand around.

"I'm afraid he's got it all wrong," the man carrying the express gun said. He was a man in his early thirties with dark hair and a cruel, square face. Both breast pockets of his faded tan shirt had a gold star design in their center. "We come on these poor critters wandering around lost, so we figured to take 'em up north and give them a nice new home."

The rustlers all snickered at the lie their leader told, but they never changed the aim of their weapons. Jim knew that both his and Dwayne's lives were in grave danger, and his mind raced to find a way out.

"I suggest you two shuck them guns and climb down before our fingers get itchy. You've got a long walk home," square face said.

Jim knew that they were dead if they complied and quite possibly if they didn't, but at least armed they could fight back. "Where is Tyler?" he wondered.

From behind him came a voice. "I'd do like Buck says," Tyler said, as if on cue. "That is, unless you want to join us." The meaning of Tyler's words struck home.

"I told you I'd fire you and set you afoot no matter where it was if I caught you stealing. You're fired, Tyler."

That caught the outlaws off guard and gave Jim a possible opportunity. Jim was glad that he was riding his buckskin, for he had been trained for mounted combat while he was living with the Cheyenne. At the end of his comment, Jim simply flopped sideways from his saddle, drawing as he fell. The hours of daily practice during his time with Two Bears had not left him. His foot caught the pommel of his saddle and his twin six-guns slid into his hands as if drawn by magnets. Dropping toward the trio of strangers, Jim hoped to catch them off guard. He partially succeeded.

The express gun belched fire and buckshot just before Jim's six-guns barked in response. Passing over the saddle where Jim had just been seated, the double load of heavy buckshot struck Tyler's mount, sending it kicking and squealing to the ground. Jim's Colts spoke in reply, and the star patterns on Buck's shirt pockets were pushed deep into his chest by two .45-caliber bullets. They found their way into his vital organs. The spongy tissue of his lungs was torn asunder by both bullet and broken rib bones, and the top of his heart was sheared off. Buck's lifeless body was flung from the saddle, and his eternal soul was greeted by the fires of hell.

Caught completely by surprise, the other two rustlers hesitated a split second too long. Dwayne was no gunman, but he pulled his own pistol and fired before the criminals recovered. A bucktoothed kid dropped his rifle and clung to the saddle of his now bucking horse, and the third rustler clutched at a wound in his abdomen and slumped from his saddle to the ground.

Jim's buckskin was the only horse, besides Tyler's now dead mount, not fidgeting or bucking. Tyler had managed to draw and fire one shot, hitting Dwayne in the back. Jim pulled himself back into the saddle and took aim at the traitor. "Drop it or die. I don't much care which." Tyler's fancy pistol fell to the dust. He had just witnessed some of the best shooting he had ever seen, and he knew that Jim was sure to hit his target if he didn't comply. "I should just shoot you, but I need you to talk."

Dwayne had managed to keep his seat and his pistol. Even with his wound, he covered "Bucktooth" and his wounded partner. Kneeing his horse over toward Dwayne, Jim started to turn toward him.

"Keep your eye on that snake boss. I'm still in the saddle." Dwayne's voice betrayed the pain he was in, but he was resolved, and Jim knew the danger of taking his eyes off a back shooter. Dwayne would have to stay in the saddle on his own, at least for the minute.

"Lock your fingers behind your head," Jim ordered Tyler.

"My leg's pinned," the thief whined. Jim simply repeated his command.

"If I have to tell you again, I'll put a bullet in both elbows so I don't have to worry about you picking up your gun."

The last sentence came out as a growl and was punctuated by Jim putting a bullet into the ground within an inch of the whiner's left elbow. There was no further argument.

Quickly dismounting and securing Tyler's wrists, Jim threw the fancy handgun into the brush after smashing the firing mechanism with a handy rock.

"I'll ask you one time. Who do you work for? I've lived with the Cheyenne, so I can make this real painful, or you can tell me now."

Jim drew his knife, and Tyler's eyes grew wide in terror as he remembered tales, some real some pure fabrication, of Indian methods of extracting vengeance or information from an enemy. He recognized the knife in Jim's right hand as a Cheyenne skinning knife.

"I don't know!" he cried. "I just make sure that nobody is around when Buck and the boys show up. Honest. Maybe the kid knows or Coleson."

Dwayne interrupted. "Boss, I ain't feeling so good."

Jim turned and saw Dwayne swaying in the saddle. Catching up the reins of the downed men's horses, Jim ordered the kid to the ground. When he noticed that the brand on one of the horses was an S Bar S, he grew even angrier at their brazenness. Coleson had died during the short interrogation, so the only one left to secure was the youngest member of the gang. Quickly tying his hands and feet, Jim mounted and started for the home ranch, leading the extra horses and Dwayne. He simply left Tyler with his leg trapped under the dead horse after quickly searching him for other possible weapons. He packed all of the outlaw's weapons onto one of the spare horses and left them without even a pocketknife. Tyler hurled obscenities at the backs of the departing pair while his young counterpart struggled frantically against his bonds.

"Can you make it?" Jim asked as soon as they were out of earshot of the outlaws. Dwayne looked pale and was still bleeding. Stopping to examine the wound, Jim plugged the hole with moss and his bandana. It was the best he could do under the circumstances.

"I'll stay in the saddle. Just lead the way." Dwayne's response was weak, but there was not much that could be done until they reached the ranch. The bleeding was almost stopped, and there was nothing left to do but head for home.

Home—that had a nice ring to it. It had been a long time since he had considered anywhere home, including the Lazy H. The thought of somewhere to call home was interrupted by a groan from his current companion. Reaching back, he caught Dwayne just as he began to slip from the saddle.

Dwayne was barely conscious, and his shirt was soaked with blood and sweat. His pale, dust-streaked face gave evidence of exactly how serious his injury was. He needed medical attention, and he needed it right away.

Jim redressed the wound and made a travois to carry Dwayne for the rest of the journey. Travel wouldn't be slowed by much, and it would be much more comfortable for Dwayne. Time was critical, but Dwayne couldn't ride any farther.

Approaching the ranch, Jim fired three shots into the air to get Whitey's attention. Whitey had lanterns lit, and the ranch yard glowed with their light when Jim drew into the yard. He was leading Dwayne's horse, which pulled the travois. The outlaw's horses were tied well behind Dwayne's Indian style ambulance.

"Dwayne's hurt bad. We came up on some rustlers, and things got ugly fast. Saddle the fastest mount we've got. He needs a doctor and now." He didn't waste words, and Whitey didn't ask questions as he switched Jim's saddle to a long-legged Appaloosa. While Whitey handled that chore, Jim picked Dwayne up as easily as if he were a child and carried him into the bunkhouse.

Coming out of the bunkhouse, Jim swung into the saddle and started out of the yard. Before he left though, he gave Whitey one final instruction. "If you see Tyler, shoot him. He's with the rustlers, and he's the one that shot Dwayne in the back." Spurring the anxious Appaloosa, Jim thundered from the yard.

Letting the horse have its head, Jim set off for town at a gallop. The horse loved to run, and he barely slowed down during the entire eight-mile trip. With every stride, Jim's apprehension grew. Dwayne looked bad before he left, and without prompt medical attention, he would die. Even with it, he might not pull through. If not...

Jim felt the old rage welling up in him. Dwayne was lying near death, if he wasn't dead already, because of thieves—thieves like those who had slaughtered his family those many years ago. Thieves who would take what an honest man or woman had worked for because they were too lazy to work themselves. Thieves who would kill and destroy for something that would never satisfy them. Raw fury began to burn in him, and he struggled to bring it under control.

Ten minutes from town, he let the Appaloosa guide itself while he prayed. He prayed for Dwayne, for wisdom for himself, and for peace in his heart. He knew that if Dwayne died and that old nature of his reared its head again, he would hunt down and kill all who were involved without mercy.

Chapter 9

When he entered town, the demons that haunted him had been vanquished again. God had granted him the peace that he had asked for.

Stopping his lathered mount in front of Dr. Halloran's office, he dropped the reins and bounded to the boardwalk. Bursting through the door of the office, he shouted for the doctor. A petite, blonde woman about forty years old came down the stairs to answer his call. Short curls surrounded her pretty face, and her brown eyes looked Jim over quickly before informing him that the doctor was out.

"Where can I find him? I have a man in dire straits, and he needs him now!" Jim's voice was strained, and he spoke rapidly.

The woman replied quickly and without being flustered. "We were invited to the Morrish ranch for dinner. I wasn't feeling well so I stayed home, but he went by himself. How bad is it?"

"Dwayne's been shot. He's lost a lot of blood. It's bad."

"Timothy leaves a horse saddled in the stable for emergencies. You take him and go get Timothy. Tell him I'll do what I can until he arrives. Go!"

She didn't wait to see if he followed her directions but started gathering anything that she thought might be needed and putting it into a black satchel. There was nothing for Jim to do but follow her instructions, so he headed out the door and to the stable behind the doctor's office.

The black gelding that was left saddled was a runner, and he turned him east out of town toward the Swinging M. He hated to leave the Appaloosa untended, but he had no choice.

The ten minutes it took to reach the Morrish ranch seemed like hours, and when he arrived, he was greeted by a throng of unfriendly punchers. Even so, he violated the custom of waiting to be asked to dismount and jumped from the back of the black before it had stopped moving. One belligerent puncher stepped up to confront him and received a solid left that tumbled him into the dust for his trouble. The rest of the punchers saw the blood on his shirt and surmised that this was a serious situation.

Drawn by the commotion, Thad Morrish stepped out onto the large front porch. His solid frame blocked much of the lamplight streaming from the house as he demanded, "What's all the racket? Who's here on Doc's horse?"

Jim didn't wait for the ranch crew to respond. "I'm sorry for the interruption, Mr. Morrish, but Dwayne's been shot. He needs the doctor right away. Is he here?"

"That no-account. It serves him right." Thad was still sore about what he perceived as Dwayne's betrayal.

"Mr. Morrish, rustlers shot him in the back. When I left him, he was in bad shape. If he dies because you're acting the fool, I'll hold you responsible!" Jim's anger was rising to the surface with his worrying about his friend. The situation would surely have blown sky high if Dr. Halloran had not stepped from the house right then.

"Thad, thank you for a wonderful meal, but it appears I have business to attend to." Without any further comment, he stepped up to a strawberry roan tied to the hitching rail and tightened the cinch. He mounted, and Jim swung astride the black he had ridden to the ranch. The two men thundered out of the yard in the direction of the S Bar S.

"You certainly have a winning way with the Swinging M, Mr. Harding. One of these times, it might just be you I have to treat. Now give me the details as best as you can. I assume that you stopped by my office and found out where I was. Donna will be on her way with all of my equipment."

"Dwayne came up on some rustlers. I came along a couple minutes later. They had the drop on us and would have killed us if we didn't move first. Tyler was with them and shot Dwayne in the back. He's lost a lot of blood and was unconscious when I headed for town. It looked bad, Doc."

"We'd better push these mounts then. I know a shorter route. Follow me."

The rest of the ride was silent except for the pounding of their horses' hooves and the creak of saddle leather. Both men had seen serious wounds before and knew the gravity of the situation.

They arrived in the ranch yard on lathered mounts and found the bunkhouse brightly lit. Whitey came out to meet them. He looked tired and worn from worry.

"She's doing all she can, but I think she needs your help, Doc. It doesn't look good, but Dwayne's still hanging on. He's tough but..." Whitey let the comment drop. "Boss, if ya got a way to, it wouldn't hurt none to talk to God about this. I'm way off his range, but you seem to know Him, and I reckon He can help if He's of a mind to."

"I've been talking to Him a lot on the trail. That Dwayne's still alive is a miracle itself. Now I guess we'll have to count on Doc's training and Dwayne's constitution. Will you take care of the horses while I go help if I can?"

"One other thing, boss. Miss Elizabeth's here helping too. She recognized Appy standing at Doc's and figured something was wrong. She came out with Mrs. Halloran to see if she could help."

"Thanks, Whitey. Cool the horses down if you would please."

Dr. Halloran worked on stemming the flow of all of the bleeding through the night. Dwayne was too weak to worry about removing the bullet right then. All that would do, according to Dr. Halloran, was start the bleeding all over again. Dwayne could live with the bullet, but he couldn't live with more blood loss.

"I've done all I can for him right now," said the doctor. "The rest is up to him. He's young and strong, but he's far from out of the woods. Keep him warm, feed him, and give him plenty of water to drink when and if he wakes up. Donna and I are going home to get some sleep. I would suggest that you do the same. I'll be back to check on him later."

Tying both of his saddle horses to the back of the surrey, Dr. Halloran and his wife set off for town as the sun began to peak over the eastern horizon. It had been a long night for everyone. Elizabeth had proven to be an adept student at treating wounds and insisted on staying at the ranch to help.

"Whitey told me a little about what happened but not much. He said that you and Dwayne had a run-in with some rustlers and Dwayne got shot. That's about all he said, but there must be more. Tyler's missing, and there are a couple of strange horses in the corral, or at least I didn't recognize them."

Jim took a couple of breaths before responding. "I fired Tyler and set him and his partner afoot. You're right about the horses. They were the rustlers' mounts. Two of them won't need them again, and the others can walk. There were four of them, counting Tyler. He's the one that shot Dwayne. I left him with his leg pinned under his horse and the youngest tied to a tree. They should be free by now and walking to their hideout or out of the country. If Dwayne doesn't make it, Tyler had better keep right on walking."

Elizabeth laid her hand on his forearm. "He'll be okay. Please, no more talk of killing or dying. I've seen too much of it already. Why can't you just put the guns away and never touch them again?"

"If good men put down their guns, those who would do evil would keep theirs and be emboldened because their victims would be defenseless against them. Until evil no longer exists, good people will need to have the means and willingness to defend themselves and others. Otherwise evil wins." Looking into her emerald eyes, he could read her desire for more gentle conversation. He smiled at her. "They did gather a couple hundred head for us. We might as well take advantage of their work. Whitey and I will ride out and bring them in this afternoon, if you'll be okay."

The conversation ended, and Elizabeth headed into the house while Jim headed for the bunkhouse to get some rest. He had been on the go for over twenty-four hours, and so had Whitey. A couple of hours of rest would have to do because that was all they could afford. Dwayne was resting easy, and they had done all they could for now.

Chapter 10

Jim awoke with a start. It was full daylight, and some sound had awakened him. Colt in hand, he tiptoed to the nearest window and peered out. Aunt Mable was climbing down from the seat of a buggy. The sound of it rolling into the yard must have dragged him from his repose. Whitey had been jostled from sleep by the sound as well and stood by the other window in the bunkhouse.

"Well, I don't reckon she's too dangerous, do you?" The old-timer yawned.

"Probably not, but I'd suggest you put some britches on before she heads this way."

Both men got dressed and checked on Dwayne's condition. Pale and unconscious, he was breathing nonetheless. Jim headed for the house while Whitey watched over Dwayne.

The kitchen door opened, and Jim was nearly drenched as Aunt Mable tossed the wash water out the door.

"Oh my, I am so sorry," yelped a startled Aunt Mable. "I ran into Dr. Halloran when he got back to town, and he told me about Dwayne. I came by to help and, well, here I am. Beth Ann is sleeping, so I thought that I'd get breakfast ready for you and Whitey. I'll keep a watch on Dwayne while you're out working too. You go get washed up, and tell Whitey to do likewise while I get coffee and breakfast going. Go on now. Get."

Shooing him off the porch, Aunt Mable headed back into the kitchen to start breakfast.

"Well, what did she say?" Whitey asked when Jim returned to the bunkhouse.

"She said for you to wash your face and your grubby paws, and drag a comb through that mop you call hair before breakfast," Jim said, "or some semblance thereof. I guess she figures two hours of sleep is more than enough, and we'd better quit loafing."

"As long as I don't have to do the cooking, that's all right by me. As far as a mop goes, you may want to drag a comb through your own."

By the time Jim and Whitey were presentable, Aunt Mable gave a shout. "Breakfast is ready. Come and get it before I throw it to the hogs!"

"I believe she'd do it too," Whitey commented. "Of course, to her way of thinking, the hogs are probably a step up from us."

"Just so she doesn't throw it to our betters, why don't you head to the house and get something to eat. I'll stay here with Dwayne."

Whitey headed for the house. A few minutes later, Aunt Mable arrived with a plate full of eggs, ham, biscuits, and a mug of hot coffee. "There's more in the kitchen if you want," she said. "You eat up, and I'll take care of Dwayne.

You and Whitey have a lot of work to do, so you shouldn't waste time lazing around here."

Whitey and Jim spent the next few weeks from before sunup until well after sundown in the saddle while Dwayne fought to hold onto life. Aunt Mable and Elizabeth took turns cooking for the men and watching over Dwayne while Jim and Whitey worked themselves and their mounts beyond exhaustion.

Dr. Halloran came out to check on Dwayne regularly. Elizabeth had Jim and Whitey help him move Dwayne to the house once he thought it was safe to do so. "It will be easier to keep an eye on him," she explained.

Chapter 11

Two hours of struggling found the bucktoothed young-ster still bound, but Tyler had managed to work his left leg out from under his dead mount. It wasn't broken but was badly bruised and swollen. He would need some assistance to walk for a while. Two of the pellets from Buck's shotgun had struck him in the right thigh, adding to his pain.

Dragging himself to his young accomplice, the two worked his bonds loose and began the slow trek to the rustler base camp. Tyler's injuries kept their progress to a slow crawl, and midnight found them still miles from the rest of the outlaw band. Hunkering down under a large blow down, the two built a fire and tried to stay warm. Neither had brought anything heavier than the light jacket that they wore, and the night had grown cold in the mountain air. Their lack of weapons was highlighted when they heard the lonely snarl of a female cougar. Whitey's bullet had killed her mate, and now she had to hunt for her cubs on her own.

Listening to her, the two rustlers built the fire higher, and fear of the big cat kept them awake the entire night.

As the sun slowly began to warm the new day, they arose from their hiding spot and continued on their way. Midmorning brought the sound of approaching hooves to the two. Hiding themselves in the brush along the trail, the pair watched the approach of several riders. Recognition brought them out of hiding to greet five members of their rustler gang.

"Hunt, Keegan, fellers, man, am I glad to see you!"

"Jubal? What's going on? Where at's Buck and Coleson? And who's this? Where's the cattle?" An unshaven man with tobacco-stained teeth fired the questions at the youngster.

"This here's Tyler. He's the one what was at the ranch. We had some trouble. Buck and Coleson are dead. You got somethin' to drink? We been without since yesterday."

Tossing his canteen to the youngster, Hunt pondered what to do next. Jubal and Tyler each took a long pull at the canteen before Jubal handed it back to Hunt. "Thanks. We was parched."

"We'd better haul these two back to camp and let the boss know what's up. Keegan and Saunders, you two double up with these two."

The outlaw band headed back the direction they had come from. They rode in silence, holding the questioning for their boss to do.

The camp was a conglomeration of tents and ram-shackle huts in a small canyon. To one side sat a large, well-maintained tent. The remainder of the huts and tents were along a small creek that ran through the center of the camp. They were all downstream of the large tent. The canyon contained a well-watered meadow where dozens of horses and a few hundred head of cattle carrying several brands grazed contentedly. The S Bar S brand seemed to be the most numerous one found on the flanks of the ill-gotten herd.

The cavalcade came to a stop in front of the large tent. A slightly taller than average blond man stepped out to meet them. He had broad, powerful shoulders that tapered to a lean waist. His jovial and almost boyishly innocent face always seemed to be smiling and belied the fact that he was a very dangerous man.

"Hunt, what's going on here? Weren't you supposed to bring in some more cattle?" He had seen the men riding double and had noted the two men that were absent but decided to wait to see what the explanation might be.

"There was trouble, boss. I'll let Jubal fill you in."

Jubal scrambled from his seat behind Keegan. He held his hat in his hand and looked at the ground. He didn't like that Hunt had dumped the telling of the story on his shoulders, and his nervousness was evident.

"Keegan, go relieve Haskell on lookout while Jubal fills us in."

Whirling his mount, Keegan disappeared in a cloud of dust. Knowing the boss didn't like it when things didn't go as planned, he was only too happy to be away from camp right now.

"Well?" The leader of the band was still smiling, but there was a hard glint in his hazel eyes.

"I don't know what happened, boss. We was getting set to push a couple of hundred head this way when some puncher rides up. We get the drop on him when up comes this other feller. Buck just smiles and covers him with the scatter, but this feller just drops off to the side of his horse and pulls both of his Colts as slick as you please. It happened so quick that Buck missed, with the scattergun! Before we can do much of anything, this feller plugs Buck twice, and the other puncher nails Coleson in the belly. Tyler's horse is down, but he manages to put lead into the one what shot Coleson before this crazy gun-slick swings back up and covers him. They took our mounts and guns, trussed us up, and left us. It took us a couple of hours to get loose. There weren't anything else to do but head back."

"And where were you during all the shooting?"

"My horse set to bucking. I almost got throwed and lost my rifle when my horse set to pitching. The puncher what Tyler shot had me covered afore I could do anything."

"Okay, Tyler, what happened? You get paid to make sure this kind of thing doesn't happen. Where did this other man come from, and why was he there? You told us it would be just you and one other man."

"He's the new ranch foreman, Jim something or other. I don't know why he was there. He was supposed to be working some other part of the ranch with Whitey."

By now all of the riders had dismounted and were standing around listening to Tyler tell his side of the story. "That's all I know," he concluded.

"Tyler, you were supposed to make sure these things don't happen. Because of your mistake, I'm out two good men and, according to Jubal, about two hundred head of cattle. You can't go back to the ranch because they know that you are with us, and you can't be seen with us because you will be recognized. You see, you are of no further use to us and, unfortunately for you, you know where our base is."

Realization struck Tyler just before the bullet. Smoke curled upward from the muzzle of the smiling blond's pistol while Tyler discovered that there is a special place in hell just for traitors. The gang leader calmly reloaded as if he had just shot a tin can or a target at the range.

"Take this garbage to one of the canyons and make sure it gets covered over well. I don't want vultures leading someone here."

"Jubal, come here."

A terrified Jubal stepped forward. "I'm sorry, boss. I didn't…"

"I don't blame you. The one that let us down has paid for his crime. What I need you to do is tell me about this gunslick. What does he look like? How tall? What color hair? That sort of thing."

Jubal gave a fairly accurate description of Jim. He missed a few details, and Jim was taller in his description than in real life, but when he was finished, the gang leader had a fairly accurate idea as to what his adversary looked like.

"One other thing, boss. His eyes was blue and cold as ice. If'n looks could've killed, you wouldn't of had to shoot Tyler. He'd of been dead already. It kinda gave me the willies."

"We'll take care of him later. Right now, you go get something to eat while I think this through. We'll probably move what we have to market and let things cool down a might before we start our next gather."

Tyler's body had been loaded up for disposal, and Jubal headed to the cook tent for some food. He hadn't realized how hungry he was until now. He didn't give much more thought to Tyler. He had proved to be a coward and a blabbermouth, so he wouldn't be missed that much.

Chapter 12

The time had finally come when Dwayne could travel safely. Whitey and Jim loaded him into a well-padded buckboard to transport him to town. The doctor wouldn't have to travel to the ranch to check up on him that way. Besides, Aunt Mable needed to get back to her boarding-house. She had left some instructions with some helpers, but she needed to get back to her own home.

The whole ranch loaded up and headed for town. Jim and Whitey needed a break and the ranch needed supplies.

The buckboard arrived in front of Aunt Mable's with its small escort and no fanfare. They moved Dwayne into Jim's old room. He would stay there while he recovered. Aunt Mable would ensure that he followed the doctor's orders, and he would be far less likely to reinjure himself under her care than out at the ranch trying to help before he was ready.

Whitey headed for the general store with a list of needs for the ranch while Jim headed for the telegraph office.

There were some things that he needed to check on and an order he needed to place.

"How can I help you?" The operator was an oldster wearing thick spectacles. What was left of his snow-white hair looked as soft as down, and his fingers were gnarled from years of operating the telegraph key. His cheery smile brightened the dimly lit office.

"I need to send a message to Broken Bow, Montana. I'd like the response sent to Aunt Mable's. Send the wire to Joshua Gordon, care of the Lazy H Ranch: 'Any new brands at the mines? Am at the S Bar S ranch in Lone Oak, Wyoming. Send three hundred head of young stock to trade for one hundred fifty market ready. Send Hank, Skipper, Flying Eagle, Daily plus four to drive market ready. Inform upon receipt. Jim Harding.' Tell no one of this message and send the response as soon as it comes in."

"I always figure the person who sends a message is the only one it concerns. Now that's a heap of sending. It'll be three dollars to do it."

Jim paid the operator and headed out the door. Unless Joshua was in town, it would be at least several hours before any response could be expected, possibly a day or more. He moseyed over to Davenport's Mercantile to help Whitey with the supply order.

Entering the cool, dim interior of the general store, Jim's nostrils were invaded by the scent of leather, wool, and hundreds of other dry goods. Whitey was at the counter going over the list with a pale-faced young man that looked quite familiar.

"Hi, Kid." Jim's greeting interrupted the two and embarrassed the younger man.

Jim approached the counter and stuck out his hand. "No hard feelings, I hope. By the way, my name is Jim."

The return grip was firm. "Bobby, Bobby Morrison. I apologize for the way I acted that night. I thought I was fast, but I never even saw your hand move, and it was over. I figured right then and there to go back to my old line of work. I'm just glad the Davenport's took me back after the way I acted."

"Well, Bobby, if it hadn't been for you that night, the missus and me would probably be residing beneath the sod. Never let it be said that Alfred Davenport forgets a thing like that." The cherubic Alfred Davenport emerged from the backroom where he had been pulling an order for another customer.

"You see, several months back we were closing up for the evening when in strolled these three strangers. One of them starts wagging his gun in my face and demanding our proceeds. One of the others grabs my lovely Rose and shoves her behind the counter too. They started making some crude comments when Bobby steps out of the back room with those fancy six-guns in his hands. We had just gotten them in, so he must have seen what was going on and loaded them up. He steps out and says, 'Leave them be.'

"The one that had been waving his pistol in my face just laughs and starts to turn on Bobby, so Bobby lets him have it. He turns on the other two and gets one of them before the last one makes a run for the door. There was a reward for the two of them, which Bobby used to buy that palomino mare of his. We gave him the pistols as a thank-you. He ran into the last of the miscreants at a tavern when he was visiting another town. The scoundrel was drunk and tried to draw on Bobby. Bobby defended himself and got a reputation. The Swinging M hired him after that."

Bobby smiled. "I guess I started believing my own press, or I read too many of them dime novels. Feeling a little too high and mighty, I guess."

"I'm glad you landed safely back on the ground," Jim replied. "Now, if you could help Whitey with the order, I'm going over to see if Aunt Mable needs anything that we can pick up for her while we are here."

"Just like a foreman to leave all the heavy lifting for some poor, ole puncher while he goes to confab with some womenfolk to see if he can scare up some more work for said overworked employee."

Jim didn't wait to hear the rest of Whitey's tirade. He knew, and Whitey knew, that there really wasn't any heavy lifting, and he would be back to help long before any loading actually got started. What Whitey didn't know was that he planned for them to stay the next night or two in town. The cattle would keep for that long, and after the way they had been pushing themselves, they could use the rest.

Jim strolled to Aunt Mable's and mounted the steps to the front porch. Stepping through the front door, he heard excited voices and followed them to parlor where he found Elizabeth, Aunt Mable, and a few other ladies deep in conversation. They failed to notice him until he cleared his throat.

"We were just finishing up at Davenport's and wondered if…"

"Oh, Jim!" Elizabeth exclaimed. We didn't hear you come in. Janie and Sally were just telling us there's a barn dance and picnic tomorrow and a box lunch on Sunday. They're having a kind of fair. I know that there is a lot of work to do at the ranch, but it seems so long since I've been to a dance, and you and Whitey have been working so hard that you need a break too. It would be nice to just enjoy the day without having to work yourself to a frazzle."

"Well I was planning on staying in town the next couple of days to make sure that Dwayne was settled in. You are the boss, so if you say to take the next couple of days off, who am I to argue?" He turned to Aunt Mable. "I was actually coming here to see if you needed anything from Davenport's. Whitey and I can bring it with us if you do."

Aunt Mable wrote out a list of some staples that she needed, adding extra flour, sugar, and dried apples to make pies for the picnic. "Tell Davenport to send some fresh rhubarb if he has some."

"Will do. Now I'd better head back before Whitey has a fit. I almost forgot—did Harpers send my laundry here, or is it still at their place?"

"Tommy picked it up, and I have it in a chest I have for just such things. You'd better get now, or Whitey will swear you abandoned him to do all the work."

"He's already done that."

Jim was off to Davenport's with his list in hand. Whitey and Bobby were just starting to load the wagon when Jim walked up. "I thought you'd already be loaded up. I guess I didn't stay gone quite long enough."

"See what I told you. Went to talk to the women-folk, hoping I'd be done with all the work by the time he got back."

The bandy-legged puncher waited for Jim as long as he could. "Well, did she send us more work to do?"

"Of course she did! Flour, apples, sugar, and rhubarb for pies plus a couple of other things. How about we load the wagon while Bobby pulls the order?"

Handing the order to Bobby, Jim set about helping Whitey load the wagon. "Don't forget the rhubarb if you've got some," he shouted at Bobby's retreating back.

"How would you like it if we take tomorrow off and loaf around town a bit?" Jim asked Whitey. "We've been doing the work of five men, and there'll still be plenty when we get back. The cows will keep for a day or two. Besides, according to the boss, there's some big shindig going on tomorrow."

"Will miracles never cease? The taskmaster is giving the poor worker some time off. Well you won't catch me refusing. Any shindig that includes Miss Mable's pies is worth attending."

They finished loading the supplies for the ranch and tossed Aunt Mable's order on top for the short trip to the boardinghouse.

Chapter13

The boarding house had grown busy during Jim's short absence. Families had started to arrive, and those who could afford it were seeking accommodations.

"Whoo-ee! It looks like we'll be lucky to sleep in the stable tonight."

"She always fills up when there's some big to-do in town." The oldster smiled. "I reckon it's her coffee. There's none better, less'n maybe it's mine."

"Yours? You don't even wash out the pot."

"Shows what you youngsters know. That's what gives it its special flavor."

Jim just rolled his eyes and remained quiet. What Whitey lacked in coffee-making etiquette, he more than made up for in hard work, dedication, and cooking ability. Besides, his coffee wasn't really *that* bad.

The two quickly unloaded Aunt Mable's order and found that she had saved a room for them. They parked the wagon next to the stable. After stabling all four of their horses, Jim picked up his laundry from his first trip to town, and the two tromped upstairs to settle in.

"I should've knowed to bring in some fresh duds for a trip to town. Here you had yours all clean and pressed and waiting for just such a thing."

"As far as long johns go, you're on your own, but you're more than welcome to borrow a clean shirt and some pants for tomorrow if you want. The shirt might be a tad loose, but I think you'll be all right."

"Well, thanks. I feel a heap better about the whole thing now. What say we stow our gear and hit the town?"

Following through on Whitey's suggestion, the two quickly stowed their gear and headed for one of Whitey's hangouts, The Rusty Nail Saloon.

"Boss, I hope you don't mind if I have one beer with the boys. I know the rule, but it's my custom, and I only drink one."

"As long as you keep a lid on it and you don't mind if I drink sarsaparilla."

"Deal."

The men placed their order and, due to what happened the last time, no one commented on Jim's order. Whitey made the rounds with his one drink and introduced the foreman to the neighboring ranch and farmhands. With the festive mood in the air, even the Swinging M hands were friendly. The sole exception was the truculent puncher who had been the recipient of Jim's left hook on their only other meeting. He glowered at the S Bar S foreman as he was introduced around.

A friendly puncher from the C&O ranch asked, "Is it true you made good on Dwayne's pay from the Swinging M? It don't seem right what Thad done."

"That's what I told him I'd do. As for Mr. Morrish, I think he was just upset. He's not used to being challenged, especially by one of his own hands."

"Conway! You calling Mr. Morrish a crook or something?" It was the Swinging M puncher with a chip on his shoulder. He had found a safe target for his embarrassment at Jim's hands. While no coward, Conway was a gentle soul.

"Tibbits, I said no such thing. I just think it's wrong for someone to not pay someone else their due."

Tibbits had a short fuse and was more than willing to light it himself if no one else would. He liked to fight dirty and would put the boots to a man after he was down and out. He was also a fair hand with a six-gun, which Conway was not.

"I say that worthless bum got better'n he deserved. He should've been set afoot and not allowed to ride. I say if you disagree with me you're calling me a liar. Now what do you say to that?"

The floor between the two was quickly vacated, and the two faced each other from just a few feet apart.

"I guess I see things different than you, but I ain't gonna draw." Conway simply turned his back and resumed his drink.

Tibbits crossed the open space between them and smashed his beer stein behind Conway's right ear, crumpling him unconscious to the floor. The gentle puncher was helpless as Tibbits started to work. Unfortunately for Conway, he was the only C&O puncher in the establishment, so he was alone.

The sadistic attacker landed several kicks and raked his spurs across his victim's ribs before help arrived. Tibbits was literally lifted off his feet and tossed aside, like a sack of grain, to land in a heap. He hadn't seen Conway's rescuer shove through the crowd like an angry bull.

"Keep 'em off me, Whitey! You can fill your hand if you think you're fast enough, or you can take your beating face-to-face." Jim's face showed his rage, and his blue eyes were like ice daggers that bore deep into his opponent's soul.

"My fight's not with you."

"It is now, Tibbits. I'll count to three. Then you either drop the belt and take your beating or fill your hand."

"I ain't no gunfighter like you, so let's just see if you can fight without them six-guns."

Deliberately, Tibbits tossed his gun belt aside. Unknown to Jim, he still retained a very sharp boot knife and thought he knew how to use it. Keeping his eyes on Tibbits, Jim stripped off his gun belt and handed it to a nearby cowboy. Tibbits grinned wickedly as he squatted and drew the knife from his boot. Both edges of the six-inch-long spear-point blade were kept razor sharp, and he held the knife in his right hand as if he had used it before.

Jim moved to his right on catlike feet. Like a big cat playing with a poisonous snake, every sense was alert. The reflexes had to be exceptional, or one strike could prove fatal. There was no retreat.

The barroom had grown silent as the combatants circled one another. A few feints by Tibbits failed to draw Jim in. Conway had recovered enough to move out of the combat zone but refused to visit the doctor until the drama before him played out.

Crouching, Tibbits launched his first attack. Thrust, hack, slash, sweep, stab—all met empty air as Jim, like a great cat, jumped and twisted, avoiding the blade. He was watching and gauging his foe, waiting for his time to strike.

Again the attack came, and again Jim danced out of the blades way. The unproductive attacks continued for several minutes. The crowd watched in awe as Jim deftly avoided being sliced to ribbons. The lightweight moccasins that he wore aided his ease of movement. A heavy boot would have slowed him, and the hard soles and stiff uppers would have impaired his balance and flexibility.

Tiring and growing frustrated, Tibbits put all he had into a slash at Jim's throat. Jim avoided the stroke and went to work. His own right hand seized his opponent's knife wrist and clamped down like an iron vise. A quick twist and a blow to the elbow with his left hand sent the knife skittering in one direction and his antagonist another. Jim's blood was up, and the beating started. Tibbits would have stood a better chance wrestling a grizzly with a sore tooth. The first few blows pulped his lips and swelled his left eye shut, and it went downhill fast from there. When he finally slumped unconscious to the floor, he had two broken ribs and countless bruises; both his eyes were swollen shut, and he had a broken wrist and nose. Some of the few areas of his body not injured were his knuckles, for he had failed to land a single blow.

"Swinging M, my fight was with Tibbits only, not the Swinging M. He was putting boots to an unconscious man, and I don't think that that is the Swinging M's style. Tough? Yes. Hard? Sometimes. But cruel and cowardly? No. Now if you'll let me, the next round is on me."

Whoops and hollers went up as the bar was swarmed. Two Swinging M hands carried Tibbits to Dr. Halloran's office and hurried back to get their free refill. More than one puncher had been on the receiving end of Tibbits's cruelty, and he was far from the favorite at the Swinging M.

"Boss, you'll go broke buying for this lot."

"Just this one time. We don't need any more headaches from Thad than we already have, and this should salve the wounded pride a little. One thing though, don't blab this to Aunt Mable or Elizabeth."

"Aw, shucks. That was at the top of my list of things to do."

"Can you stay out of trouble if I head over to Mickey's?"

"Me? If I recollect right, I was sipping peacefully on my one and only drink when some hothead drinking sarsaparilla popped a cork, or did I miss something?"

Jim had to laugh. When Whitey was right, he was right. He pulled out some money and paid for the promised round of drinks, receiving handshakes and slaps on the back from all.

"Whitey, when you're done here, meet me at Mickey's, and I'll buy you dinner. We need to talk."

He left the saloon and headed for the restaurant. Seeing Thad and Dean Morrish seated by themselves in the busy diner, he walked over to their table. Thad looked at him curiously while Dean just glowered.

"Mr. Morrish, may I join you for a moment? There is something you need to know, and I believe it should come from me."

Still curious, Thad waved him to an empty chair. "What's on your mind?"

"Thank you. I'll be brief so that you can get back to your meal. You have a man working for you named Tibbits?"

"Yes. Somewhat quarrelsome but a fair hand most of the time. Why?"

"He started to put the boots to a C&O hand named Conway. Conway was out cold and had his back turned when Tibbits clubbed him with a beer mug. I intervened. I apologize to you for costing you another hand. He will live, but he had to be carried to the doctors. I believe you would have stopped it yourself had you been there."

Dean was on his feet, but Thad restrained him with a gentle touch.

"You shot him?"

"No, sir. If I had done that, he would be dead, not injured. He pulled a knife on me, and I simply thrashed him. You had other hands there that witnessed it. I came to you because I don't want trouble between the Swinging M and the S Bar S. I explained to all who were there that my dispute was with Tibbits and not the Swinging M."

"Gotta give you credit. You got guts coming to me after beating one of my men. Most would have high-tailed it out of town instead. I'll give it some thought."

"That's fair enough. Thank you."

Jim rose, and the Morrishes resumed their meal, having a new topic for thought and discussion. Finding a partially empty table, he sat down. A weary but smiling Joe saw him and hurried over.

"I see you're in town. Any chance Elizabeth's here too? I could sure use the help if she is."

"I think she's at Aunt Mable's. If she isn't helping with baking pies, she may be willing to help out. Do you have someone to send for her?"

"Yeah. Tommy's helping today to earn some extra cash for tomorrow. I'll send him. Gotta run."

"Hey, Joe. Why Mickey's instead of Joe's?"

Joe laughed. "I won it in a poker game from Mickey Silvers. I've been too busy or too lazy to bother changing it." Off to the kitchen he flew.

Whitey walked in a few minutes later and spotted Jim and headed his way. He noticed Thad and Dean as he walked over.

"They could be trouble when they hear what you done. Their boys won't start nothing without their say-so. They ain't that fond of Tibbits but if Thad says to."

"They already know, and they seem peaceful enough."

"They already know?"

"Sure. I saw them when I came in and talked to them about it to head off trouble. I thought it would be better if they heard it from me, rather than some drunken cowhand with a distorted memory."

The waitress interrupted their conversation. She smiled as she took their order and poured coffee, and then she headed off to the next table to take their order.

"Whitey, what do you know about the situation here? Are other ranches losing stock or just us? Is it large scale or just penny ante? Any ideas about where they're selling it at?"

"We been hit the hardest, but the Swinging M is losing some stock too. I reckon we must be closest to their market—been losing more since about two months after Sam got killed. Don't know much more."

Their food arrived, and they dug in with gusto. Typical of Western men, the communication ended until the food was gone. Jim mulled over the information he had been given but didn't come to any conclusions. He might learn more when he got an answer to his wire.

"The goldfields up north would take beef with no questions asked. They'd take horses and mules the same way. That could be their market and would put the S Bar S in the perfect location to fill their needs," Jim thought out loud.

"I betcha you're right, but what do we do? You and me can't go after 'em alone and not without some idea what we're up against. There ain't no law out here but what a man makes for himself. Not even no town marshal."

"I sent for some help. It'll be a week or two, but they will come. Until then we just keep working—that and talk to the other ranchers. They know you. Can you arrange it?"

"They'll all be in town for the festivities tomorrow. How about before things kick off?"

"That sounds great. Just tell me the time and location."

"I'll set it for ten o'clock here. Joe's got a room for just such meetings."

Whitey headed out the door to make the arrangements while Jim paid for the meal. Elizabeth was entering just as Jim headed out the door. Catching her attention, he quickly informed her of the meeting they set for the next morning.

"Are you sure I should be there?"

"You are the owner. I think it's important."

"All right then. I've got to go help Tammy now. She's been waiting tables all day by herself." She was off to put on an apron and help out.

Jim walked the busy street, greeting people as he went. Families were hustling about, getting ready for the next day's events. Ranch crews were arriving in groups of two or three, leaving their day's work early. One wagon rolled by with a huge hog loaded in one crate and more than a dozen fat squealing piglets in another. There was a fattened C&O steer in one of the holding pens at the edge of town near the butcher shop. The huge steer showed that the Olsons knew something about raising beef. Both the D/C and Swinging M had several half-grown calves in the other pens.

The town square was being transformed with decorations, and plank tables were being erected around its outer edges. Two huge fire pits were dug, and smoke was beginning to rise from a newly kindled fire in the larger one.

To the east of town, makeshift corrals were being erected for some of the next day's events. The carnival-like atmosphere was contagious, and Jim soon found himself working alongside men from every ranch and farm in the area on whatever needed to be done. Behind the butcher shop, there was a single gunshot, and a short time later, the C&O steer, now skinned and quartered, made his way in a wagon to be the guest of honor at the larger of the two fire pits. They would start the hog in the early morning hours. Whitey found him helping put up one of the corrals.

"All set for the morning. I think everyone will show."

"Good."

The men pitched in to finish the corrals and moved to help with other things needing done. During that time, Jim learned about some of the next day's activities. Calf roping, shooting contests, chicken pulls, horse races, and more were on tap. There was a huge afternoon picnic and barn dance that evening as well. All were welcome.

"Too bad we didn't bring Appy in. He's the runningest horse I ever sat."

"Thad's got one that'd give him a run for the money, a big buckskin stud. Depends who he's got riding him, but he'd make it a race. Want me to bring in Appy in the morning? I can have him here in plenty of time for the race."

"If you'll ride for the ranch, let's make it a race. Would you mind bringing Buck in too? I think I'll give that chicken pull a try."

"Sure thing. I'll leave early and be back afore things get started."

When the sun set, the town had been transformed into one giant fairground ready for Saturday's festival to begin.

Jim and Whitey headed to Aunt Mable's to turn in. The town was still bustling with activity, but the work was done, and it was mostly cowhands blowing off steam. Along the way they met Dr. Halloran, who gave them an update on Tibbits.

"No doubt he deserved it but I've never seen a man beaten so thoroughly without being dragged by his horse or trampled by a bull."

"I've seen Preacher deal out as good or better in his day, all the while quoting the Old Testament."

Whitey didn't miss the conversation, and when Jim stripped off his shirt later to wash up before turning in, there was no missing the scars.

"Had my suspicions. You're Harding from the Lazy H up Montana way. Should've guessed right off the way you handle yourself in a fight and talk to God and such. Didn't really think about it til you mentioned Preacher and I seen them scars."

"Do me a favor and don't spread it around. Too many wannabe gun-slicks want to prove themselves at my expense. That weighs heavy on a man."

No more was said, and they turned in for the night.

Chapter 14

Early the next morning, Whitey set off on his errand, and Jim headed for the telegraph office after his early morning workout. He wasn't expecting a reply quite yet, but one never knew. As expected, there was no response yet.

Continuing his stroll through town, he noticed more than one cowhand suffering the effects of their previous night's revelry. One young puncher staggered from an alley holding his head, only to turn and run a few steps back into the alley, dry-heaving as he went and swearing that he would never touch the "devil's brew" again. Most of the older punchers had headed back to their respective camps long before they had reveled enough to suffer such results.

Jim was enjoying the coolness of the morning. The quiet gave him time to think, pray, and meditate. This morning, he had a lot to think about. He had let that old nature out just a little in his dealing with Tibbits. Sure he could rationalize it by saying that Tibbits deserved it, but he knew he had gone far beyond what was needed. He surely would have killed him if he had touched a gun.

His meandering took him to a small, quiet clearing near the stream where barrels had been filled with drinking water the night before. Seating himself beside a large cottonwood, he took out a Bible he carried and began to read.

A soft footfall from the brush behind him interrupted his reading. Nothing in his adult life gave him the opportunity to ever be completely off guard. Slipping his right-hand Colt into his hand, he rolled to his left and laid prone, gun in his hand, facing the direction of whoever was quietly approaching. It was a precaution, which proved to be completely unnecessary.

The owner of the soft footfalls was also the owner of long, soft blonde curls that framed a very pretty, young face. The blue eyes that scanned the area held a youthful joy, and unlike Jim's own icy blue eyes, they were like two deep blue pools of clear, cool water. Slightly over five feet in height, she was one of the prettiest women he had ever seen. Rising to his feet, he holstered his revolver.

"Oh my! Am I really that scary that you need a gun? I must look a fright in the morning to scare a man so."

"No, ma'am, quite the contrary. As for scaring a man, as pretty as you are, a man would have to be plumb loco not to be at least a little scared of you."

"So which one are you?"

"Maybe a little of both. By the way, I'm Jim."

"Are you Jim from the S Bar S? Do you work with Dwayne? I haven't seen him since he went to work out there. Is he hiding from me?" Her voice bubbled with excitement.

"Since I don't know your name, I can't possibly answer that last question, but I am working at the S Bar S with Dwayne, if you can call what he does working."

"I'm Cheryl Cochran. Dwayne usually dances with me at the barn dances, but I hadn't seen him. I didn't know if he was coming. You know, he's not scared of me."

"Well that doesn't surprise me. I know for a fact that he is loco. He is in town, but I don't think he'll be up to dancing. Haven't you heard what happened to him? I thought the whole county would have known by now."

Her eyes grew wide, and her voice trembled slightly. "What happened? Is he all right?"

Jim explained as simply as he could that Dwayne had been shot and was recovering slowly. He told her that he was at Aunt Mable's resting. "He's a good man, and I'm glad to be working with him. You said your name is Cochran. Are you David Cochran's daughter?"

"No, silly. David is my big brother. My folks died a couple of years back, and he and Debbie, his wife, took me in. Do you think Aunt Mable will let me see him?"

"You would have to ask her, but she might allow it, although he's not much to look at. He won't be up to dancing tonight, but I'll bet a visit from a girl as pretty as you sure will brighten his day."

She waved and hurried gracefully toward town. Jim smiled after her. He hoped that she might be able to visit. Aunt Mable was very strict about her "no women in the men's area of the house" rule, but she might make an exception due to Dwayne's injury; besides, she could always chaperone.

He picked up his Bible and started to read again. He smiled as he sat back down beside the old cottonwood. She sure was pretty, and if she had her cap set for Dwayne, he'd better be scared, or he was for sure going to be married.

Later, he headed back to the boardinghouse for a late breakfast and to see how Dwayne was progressing. He also wanted to be prepared for his meeting with the ranchers in the valley. There were a few questions he wanted to find out the answers to before meeting some of the ranchers for the first time. Personalities had to be considered in this type of situation. Thad was a known quantity, but the others were unknown to him. He wanted to make sure that Elizabeth was ready too.

Aunt Mable met him at the door. "You know my rule and you send that young girl here to visit Dwayne anyway? Well, I didn't have the heart to refuse her. She's a sweet girl, but next time we'll have to get Dwayne to the parlor if she is going to visit."

"I'm sorry about that. I didn't know what to tell her other than to ask you and remind her about your rule. I figured that being visited by such a pretty girl might just get him to feeling better quick." Changing the subject, he continued. "Is there any breakfast left? I haven't eaten yet, and my stomach is starting to wonder if my throat has been cut."

Aunt Mable managed to scare up some leftover hotcakes and cooked some bacon and eggs to round out breakfast for Jim. He helped himself to some of the coffee on the stove and continued to think about his fast-approaching meeting with the area ranchers. He gathered some paper and a pencil stub to write some notes to help arrange his thoughts and ideas for the gathering. Aunt Mable helped him some with her knowledge of the ranchers and their personalities.

He hadn't realized how late it was getting to be until he glanced up at the clock. It was already nine thirty, but he had something of an agenda for the ten o'clock meeting. A few minutes later, Elizabeth entered the dining room.

She nervously anticipated the ranchers' council. They both hoped that it would prove beneficial for all of the ranches in the valley.

"Well, we'll be early, but shall we head for Mickey's? There's no sense in delaying."

Side by side, the two strolled toward Mickey's. Jim went over what he hoped to accomplish at the meeting as they neared the restaurant. He wasn't quite sure how he would be received by the local ranchers but knew that an attempt had to be made to stem the rustling or the entire valley would be robbed. Lone Oak had a chance to become a fine place to live and raise a family, but it needed stability and the rule of law to survive. He knew of other small ranching communities that had been driven under by unchecked rustling or vigilante justice. He wanted to stop both.

Joe met them at the door and ushered them into his meeting room where Thad and Dean were already seated and their foreman stood behind them. Frank Baxter was tough and competent. That Thad had him as foreman was a stroke of luck. He had a reputation for thinking things through before acting and then following through completely.

Exchanging greetings, they waited for the remainder of the ranch representatives to make their appearance. Jim had met some of the ranch hands but hadn't met the owners of the other two ranches yet. Thad had chosen the head of the table, as was his custom. He was still used to being in charge of everything he was involved in. This could prove tricky for Jim. He would have to use his head instead of his fighting ability if he wanted things to work. Somehow he had to win Thad over.

Next in were Clyde and Oliver Olson. The family resemblance was obvious. They were solid, square-jawed men with a slight hint of gray showing through their otherwise coal-black hair. They each greeted Thad and Dean and shook hands with Jim. They seemed a little dubious about Elizabeth being there but said nothing. They might appear slow and somewhat uncertain, but Jim had little doubt that they both missed very little of what happened around them and were highly intelligent. When they spoke, there would be a reason—and not just to hear themselves talk.

David Cochran made his appearance just before ten o'clock. His foreman followed the blond rancher closely. He turned out to be the puncher who had held Jim's gun belt for him during Tibbits's beating. "Jake Kellogg" was how he was introduced. After shaking hands, he wisely decided against mentioning the previous evening's events.

Whitey came in right behind the D/C foreman and stood to one side. He was more than a little interested in how his foreman was going to pull these strong, independent men together to form a coalition of any kind. These men knew each other but worked independently and were proud of their own brand.

At ten o'clock, Jim started. "I suppose we should get started. Thanks to all of you for coming. I asked Whitey to invite you here to talk about a problem that is plaguing the S Bar S and may be starting to fan out. As you may know, I am working at Miss Davis' ranch as foreman. With as small of a crew as we have, there has been a large loss of cattle, and some horses have gone missing as well. It started about a year ago when Sam was killed and has continued to be a problem."

Thad interrupted. "Way I heard it, one of your own hands was involved. Sounds to me like you have a problem, not us."

Jim could see the other ranchers following Thad's train of thought and wanted to finish getting his ideas out before the other ranchers simply said, "Deal with your own problems. We have our own to handle."

"True enough. Tyler was involved, but he is no longer in our employ. He was caught and set afoot with one of his partners. That was the day that Dwayne was shot. Since that time, Whitey and I have been doing all that we can to move S Bar S cattle into areas where we can keep a better tab on them. We believe that the stolen cattle are being pushed to the mining camps up north where there won't be any questions asked about brands, and beef is in high demand. If that is the case, then the rustlers won't stop until they have cleared out the entire valley, or they are cleared out themselves."

Jake spoke up this time. "You set two of the rustlers afoot instead of hanging them? Sounds like the old oak tree in town would have taught a stronger lesson."

Several of the men muttered in agreement.

"I don't believe in lynching. Besides that, Dwayne had been shot, and there wasn't time to haul them in for trial."

"Could have just shot 'em."

"That would have been murder since they were unarmed when we left them. We're getting off the trail just a little. Thad, we found quite a few head of your stock on our range and started moving them back to their home range. As S Bar S cattle disappear from that range, your cattle will drift that way, making them easy pickings for the rustlers. Your men don't work Miss Davis' range, so they would hardly even have to cover their tracks. What I am proposing is that we all work together to wipe out the rustling operation in the area before it grows large enough to wipe all of us out. I've seen it happen to small ranching communities before."

The door from the main dining room opened, and in stepped the telegraph operator. "I knew that this was important, so I figured I'd bring it by. I kinda thought it might have something to do with this get-together." He handed the telegram to Jim and headed back out the door.

"Your timing could not have been better. Thanks. Gentlemen and lady, I contacted some people I know up in Montana to inquire about cattle movements. This is the response. I suppose we'll all learn about it together." Opening the telegram, Jim skimmed over it before reading out loud. "'Multiple brands from Wyoming. S Bar S most prevalent. Swinging M in numbers with small numbers of others. Multiple brands on horseflesh too.'"

A couple of the men started to swear but stopped when they remembered Elizabeth's presence. Thad spoke up. "All right then, we have a problem. Just how do you propose to fix it? I say we hang 'em where we find 'em!"

Mutters of agreement started to grow, and Jim knew what it could lead to. Vigilante justice wasn't the answer, but these men lived by an old code: hang them high. So he addressed the men again.

"It might have been the way to do things years ago but not now. Now we need to bring them in and try them. If the law finds them guilty, their punishment can be dealt out to them then. What I propose is that we hunt for the trails they use to move the cattle and close them down. The group that Dwayne and I ran into was only four strong counting Tyler. But the way they talked, it is certainly a bigger operation than just them. Working in groups of three or four, we should be able to capture the rustling parties and bring them in for trial. If they fight, three or four should be able to hold their own until help arrives or the rustlers pull out. The S Bar S doesn't have enough punchers on hand to work the ranch and hunt rustlers. To be honest, we need your help.

"Thad, you have the biggest ranch in the area. I would imagine the most punchers and the most to lose. I also believe that your herd is the next target for the rustlers, so I was hoping that you might be willing to give us a few men on loan for a week or two."

"We'll need to build a jail or something to hold them if we catch any," Thad responded. "Let me think it over." It made sense for him to provide some hands, but he wanted to think it over before he committed. "Why don't we enjoy the festival today? There'll be time enough to hunt skunks later."

Mutters of agreement rose. The gathering broke up without any solid agreements, but Jim thought that if he could get Thad on board, the rest would follow his lead.

Whitey pulled Jim to the side after the group dispersed. "I got Appy and Buck in Aunt Mable's stable. They're both fit as a fiddle and ready to run. We should have a grand time today." He proved to be almost prophetic in his prediction.

Chapter 15

The town had come to life, and the sounds of celebration greeted their ears when they headed back to Aunt Mable's. The aroma of roasting meats filled the air. Several families were walking around town, and dozens of children ran and played in the dusty street while the stray dogs from town chased and played with them. Cowhands raced their horses up and down the streets where it was safe, and clusters of women and girls of all ages gathered talking about the upcoming picnic and dance.

The two men headed back to Aunt Mable's to get ready for the day's events. Whitey had taken the time to gather some clothes for the festivities while he was at the ranch, and the two men spent little time in preparation. Aunt Mable saw them coming from their room.

"You two got here just in the nick of time. I was trying to figure how to get my pies to the picnic, and here you are. I kinda figured if I sent them with Tommy, they might not make it all the way before he and some of his friends helped themselves. Seeing as how Whitey is shy on friends and I don't think you would help yourself to these pies before the picnic. Would you two mind hauling them for me?"

"I ain't shy on friends." Whitey smiled. "Just selective."

"Of course we'll carry them for you." Jim volunteered before he knew exactly how many pies they were to carry. Aunt Mable had spent the entire previous afternoon and half the night baking, and the task took two heavily loaded trips to complete. "I can see why Tommy would have helped himself. He would have needed the extra energy to carry all of these."

"I would've warned you, but I figured she'd have roped us into it some other way."

Wandering around town, Jim found a schedule of events for the day. The horse race was the biggest event except for the dance and was set to happen just before supper. A second crate of piglets arrived bearing a sign "Greased pig contest".

"What in the world is a greased pig contest?" he wondered aloud.

"You ain't never seen one before? You're just gonna have to watch and see. The kids love it. Their mamas ain't so sure about it." Jim would learn why after the noon meal.

Just before noon, the whole town started toward the town square for the start of the fun. Jim and Whitey fell in with the rest. While the men and boys had been busy erecting the many corrals, tables, and other temporary structures around town, the women and girls had been busy preparing enough food to feed the town for a week. Even with all of the tables, it wasn't easy to find a place to sit, but they managed. After the meal, one of the townsmen stood up on a raised platform to announce the beginning events.

"Folks, when you're done eating, we can all head over to the small corral for the first event. All of you kids ready?" A huge roar of excited children's voices greeted the announcement. "All right! Then let's get started. Before we get started though, I need some fellers to do the honors and flood the arena with those barrels of water around it."

Dozens of cowhands and farmers jumped to help, and the small corral was converted to a huge mud pit. The piglets that had been brought to town were covered with lard and released into the pen where they ran around squealing with no idea what was next.

"All of you up to age twelve can join in this time around. From thirteen to sixteen, you're up next," the announcer boomed.

Children seemed to appear out of the woodwork and climbed into the pen for the fun. At the signal to start, they darted to and fro after the squealing greased piglets. Just as one child would think they had one of them caught, the piglet would wiggle, and the coating of lard would prove too much for the child. Mud flew everywhere as children and piglets alike ran, splashed, and slipped in the mud. The children squealed with delight as the piglets squealed in fright. After about twenty minutes, one little boy about eight years old managed to fall in the mud with a squirming piglet in his lap. He secured a hold on the baby pig that looked to be almost as big as he was and pulled it and himself into the winner's area. Whoops and hollers went up as the mud-covered boy raised his hands in victory, and the piglet scurried back off to join his friends.

"You were right, Whitey. That was something I had to see for myself. It sure looked like fun. I can see why the kids love it and their mothers don't. It'll take a dozen washings to get all of the mud out of those clothes."

The games continued with young and old joining in. The kids enjoyed sack races, three-legged races, and a dozen other games, while the adults participated in more daring activities. Calf roping didn't sport the little bawling for their momma calves of later rodeos but included wild, half-grown steers weighing three hundred pounds or more. It took all a man had to throw one and tie the legs. Several cowhands were kicked or bowled over themselves, only to have the steer they roped free itself and chase its former captor to the fence. This met with howls of laughter from the watching punchers and several shouts of advice. Conway proved to be a very competent roper. The quiet C&O puncher roped, threw, and tied his calf a full three seconds faster than the next fastest hand.

The fun continued with more than a dozen farm and ranch hands lining up for the chicken pull. The Heinemanns provided dozens of hens that were no longer laying eggs for the race. Six hens were partially buried along a line in one of the corrals. Their heads and necks were left above ground to protest their burial and flop around freely. The racers would ride their mounts along the line and pull as many chickens as they could from the ground as fast as possible. The squawking, flopping chicken heads would test the riding ability, nerve, and coordination of the riders as well as the steadiness of their mounts.

The first cowhand raced his mount toward the line of hens, only to have his horse shy when the first hen cackled loudly and swung her head toward the approaching threat. The horse sidestepped to the left while his rider flew to the right. Apparently the horse saw no reason to get any closer to the writhing thing in the dust and raced to the farthest corner from the struggling hen. The good-natured cowhand rose from the dust unhurt and gathered his mount to the laughter and applause of the watching crowd.

The spectacle continued, with most of the hands fighting their mounts to stay on course and most of the hens keeping their heads. One farmhand riding a huge plow horse plodded into the arena and trotted his mount forward. The plow horse was long used to chickens running around underfoot, so it was completely at ease. However, as the hand leaned over to grab the first hen, the cinch slipped slightly, and he slid completely under his horse. Even in this awkward position, he did grab and pull the first hen he came to. The horse was used to chickens but not to inverted riders, so the huge mare stood stationary while the young farmhand dropped to the ground beneath her. He climbed from under her belly and held up the hen he had secured, and with a sheepish grin on his face, he took a bow.

Jim had retrieved Buck from the stable and was ready to ride out. Buck had been trained to allow his rider to ride in any number of positions and was unflustered by movements around his feet. The first hen was replaced, and Jim galloped Buck into the corral and toward the line of the hens. Dropping to the side of his horse, he hooked his knee around the horn with the ease of long practice. Buck pounded toward the line of hens, and Jim began to snatch them from the ground with his right hand and secure them in his left. All six hens were pulled from the ground and handed to the judge sitting on the top rail of the fence. The hens would be plucked and added to the menu the following day. The crowd applauded the exceptional display of horsemanship.

Next up was the bronco-riding contest. Several unbroken horses were brought to the largest corral where they were blindfolded and secured while the riders drew straws to see who rode which horse. When the contest started, the object was to be the last man on his horse.

The Swinging M had several hands entered in this contest, and David Cochran rode for the D/C. The C&O had a few hands join in as well. When all had mounted, the blindfolds were removed, and the horses and crowd went wild. The cheering of the crowd only urged the mustangs to try all the harder to dislodge their riders. One by one the horses tossed their respective "busters" into the dust. This proved to be somewhat dangerous as the unseated rider had to dodge the flying hooves of the still bucking mounts while he dashed to the safety of the top rail of the surrounding corral. It seemed a miracle that only a few bruises were received in all of the confusion.

The dust settled slightly as the number of still-seated riders diminished. David Cochran was one of the last to lose his seat, and he hurried to the fence rail as the last two riders continued to cling to their particular mounts. They looked like rag dolls tied to the pitching, twisting backs of the wild horses they sat. Then there was one. Jim recognized him as he fought the horse under control. Give him credit—Dean Morrish sure could ride. He joined the crowd in cheering for the spectacular ride.

The final event was about to begin, and each of the ranches brought their entry to the line. Several cowhands also lined up with their favorite mounts to join in. Whitey arrived astride Appy, and Frank Baxter rode to the line atop a long-legged chestnut that pranced about with anticipation. The course was a one-and-one-half-mile run out to a tree halfway to the Swinging M, where the riders would turn and head back to town for the finish. There was a judge stationed at the tree to ensure that all got that far before turning around.

When the contestants were ready, the starting judge fired a shot from his pistol, and the race was on. All of the cowhands spurred their mounts into a dead run and soon were ahead of both Whitey and Frank. Both of their horses had to be held in check to keep them from charging off at top speed. It was a three-mile race not a sprint, and the two more experienced riders knew to hold some reserve for the final dash to the finish line. Whitey was the lighter of the two, but Frank was an excellent horseman himself and was determined to make a race of it.

Within the first mile, one of the cowhands was overtaken, and soon the rest would fall behind as well. Appy and the chestnut remained within a few yards of each as they passed the turning point and began to head back toward town. There was only one horse ahead of them now, and that was a smooth-running black ridden by a D/C hand. Three quarters of a mile from town, the black fell behind, and it was now a two-horse race.

Whitey held Appy in check until the finish line was within a few hundred yards. Frank had pushed the chestnut hard to stay ahead of Whitey, which was what Whitey had hoped for. Letting the appaloosa have his head, the reserve of energy and his natural love for running saw him gain on the tired chestnut with each stride.

The two horses pounded into town neck and neck. Inexorably the Appaloosa eased ahead of the chestnut and was a full length ahead of his rival when they crossed the finish line. Frank's extra weight and trying to stay ahead of Whitey had made the difference. The remainder of the field crossed the line in a far more scattered and less dramatic fashion.

Whitey led the Appaloosa up to the judge's seat where Whitey was declared the winner and therefore was to be the first in line for dinner that evening. The ten-dollar purse was a nice bonus too. Jim met him nearby and heartily congratulated him.

"It was good they had Frank up there instead of Joshua. He got throwed a couple of days ago and wasn't able to ride today. He rode for them last year and must be twenty-five pounds lighter than Frank. He knows how to get the most out of his mount too. Don't know if I could've beat him."

"Why don't you go get ready to lead the parade to the table, and I'll cool Appy down for you. Save me a seat if you can."

Jim took the reins from Whitey and started walking the weary mount to cool him off. Frank joined him walking the big chestnut. They walked along silently for a few minutes before the Swinging M foreman spoke up.

"How you been, Jim?"

"Not too bad, Frank. It's been a few years. When did you move down this way?"

"I been with Thad for about two years now. He'd die of apoplexy if he knew who you were. He thinks that this here valley is all there is, and he's the big auger. He does well, but sometimes he pushes a little harder than he needs to just to show who is boss—about the same as anywhere else, I reckon."

"Have you noticed any loss of stock? We've been pushing what Swinging M we find back home."

"There's been some, and it's been on the increase. I think you've got the idea though. We need to band together to stop it."

The two men walked past The Rusty Nail and paid no attention to the stranger standing near the door. There were dozens of strangers in town for the barn dance. He, on the other hand, was paying very close attention to them. As soon as they had passed, he finished his drink with a gulp. He knew who Frank Baxter was and recognized Jim from Jubal's description of him. Walking to his horse, he tightened the cinch while watching the two ranch foremen talking in such a friendly fashion. This was information that he had to get back to his boss. If the ranches teamed up to drive them out, the rustlers were finished.

Hunt met several members of the gang that were heading into town to enjoy the celebrations only a few miles out of town. He pulled the leader aside to fill him in on the developments.

"That gunfighter that killed Buck and got Coleson killed was talking to the foreman of the Swinging M. If they get organized, that could be bad."

The gang had pushed what cattle and horses they had up to the mining camps and sold it before returning to the Lone Oak area. A cowhand that had been passing through the area had delivered word of the celebration to them. Jubal stayed in camp, but the rest of the rustlers decided to attend and have some fun. Their leader also thought it might be a good way to learn of any new developments in the area. He wanted to meet this gunfighter for himself as well. It was always a good idea to learn as much about your enemy as possible to defeat them.

"We'll just have to see what is going on. Relax and enjoy yourself tonight, but keep your ears open and make sure that everyone stays out of trouble." The smile never left the face of the killer. As was always the case, he felt supremely confident that he was far smarter than his adversary. "Just so we don't raise any eyebrows, let's drift in in small groups. You take four or five of the boys in with you, and I'll divide the rest up and send them in about five or ten minutes apart. We'll all gather back up and head out in the morning."

Hunt trusted the planning of his leader, so he called out four names, and they all headed back to town to enjoy the evening. Ten minutes after they arrived in town, a second wave of rustlers arrived, and so it went until all twenty-seven of them found their way into town. Most headed straight for The Rusty Nail, which was doing a booming business on this evening. Some headed to the huge feast to enjoy a meal unlike what they could get in their camp. They went unnoticed as they mingled with the town folks and visitors. Nobody questioned where anyone came from, and all were welcome.

One of the men that came in with the last group was the bug-eyed outlaw named Keegan. He felt that staying close to the boss made him important, so he tried to stay close as long as the boss wasn't upset about something. When that happened, he preferred to be as far away as possible.

Strolling around the edges of the picnic area, Keegan stiffened and turned his back. Jim and Frank had returned to the picnic earlier and were seated on the far edge of the gathering enjoying their meal. They didn't pay any attention to the arriving guests, so they failed to notice the bug-eyed Keegan or his actions.

Grabbing the outlaw leader's shirtsleeve, he led him out of eyesight of the guests at the tables.

"This better be good."

"I think I know the fella that shot Buck. If it's who I think it is, he could be real trouble. His name's Jim Harden, Haring, or something like that, and he's trouble. He knows me too, so I'm heading back to camp. I'll fill you in when you get there, if that's all right by you?"

"We don't need trouble, so you head out but before you go. Which one was he?"

"He's sitting with the Swinging M foreman. Icy blue eyes that could bore right through a man. Wearing a blue shirt and sitting almost straight across the square."

"All right then, you get out of here. I'll expect more information when I get back to camp. Maybe I can learn a little about him myself tonight."

Keegan hurried to his horse and was gone from town in a matter of minutes.

The sound of fiddles being tuned up hurried the last few diners into finishing their meals in just a few bites. Many hands made light work of moving the makeshift tables from the town square, and the huge livery barn was opened to accommodate musicians and dancers alike. Torches and lanterns were lighted, and benches replaced the tables around the edges of the square.

When the music started, the usually boisterous cow-punchers and farmhands were suddenly out of their element and seemed incapable of making any moves. The young men from town stepped forward to find dance partners while the cowboys watched. Townsmen were used to being around women while their wild counterparts rarely saw, let alone talked to, those of the fairer sex. The music played, and couples whirled to the beat, laughing merrily.

Jim watched the dancers spin past as he talked to Frank and Whitey about his theory about the rustling. Jake joined them and was glad to have some input. His idea was still to hang the rustlers where they found them, but he was willing to listen and pass the information to his employer.

"Do you think Thad will throw in with us or wait until the S Bar S is empty and they start on the Swinging M in earnest? If he waits, it could be too late."

Frank gave the question some thought before he replied. "I can't speak for him, but I will speak to him. What you're saying makes sense, but you didn't make him real happy with you the last few times you had dealings with him or his hands. He listens to me most of the time, but he is the boss."

"I can't ask for more than that. Now, why don't we follow his advice and enjoy the rest of the evening."

The music was starting again, and Frank moved off to talk to some other people. Whitey grinned like a mischievous schoolboy and headed off to find a dance partner. He whirled by with Cheryl Cochran as his partner. Whitey sure was full of surprises.

When the music stopped, he rejoined Jim on the sidelines. "One advantage to getting to be my age is that you been through enough, so's asking a pretty girl to dance ain't quite so scary as it is for you youngsters." He smiled as the musicians began their next song and was off to have another whirl. He was actually pretty light on his feet and danced rather than clomped around the dance floor like most Western men.

Aunt Mable found Jim as the next song began and dragged him onto the floor. His mother had taught him to dance as a child, but he did it so rarely that he was self-conscious about his steps. His partner talked about anything and nothing, and he slowly relaxed and began to enjoy himself as he moved his feet to the music. By the time the dance was over, he felt at ease and asked for a second dance.

"Sorry but I have a full dance card tonight." Aunt Mable was off to find some other poor cowboy to dance with and make feel at ease. She always found those who were too timid to ask someone to dance and made sure that they had fun. It was no wonder everyone called her "Aunt" Mable.

Jim sat back down and was soon joined by Tommy. "Why aren't you out there?" he asked. He had noticed the youngster earlier trying to muster the courage to talk to some girls his age. It appeared that he was still trying.

"You ain't neither. Who needs girls anyway? They just try to stop you from having fun."

"I don't know about that, but it seems like it's more fun to dance with them at a barn dance than to dance without them." Jim was remembering being about Tommy's age and being completely unsure about what made girls tick. As a matter of fact, he still didn't know, and he was pretty sure that no man alive did.

Tommy laughed a little at the joke. "But what if they say no? Ain't that embarrassing?"

"There are a lot of things that are embarrassing. Maybe she'd be embarrassed if you didn't ask. Did you ever think of that? Why don't you go ask that girl you've been watching all night? What's her name anyway?"

"Denise Davenport. She's the prettiest girl I ever seen. What if she says no?"

"Then you turn to her friend and ask her. One of them is bound to say yes eventually. I'll tell you what, you go ask her, and I'll go and ask Miss Davis. She's one of the prettiest girls I've ever seen."

"That ain't no fair. She likes you. All of the boys like Denise, and she knows it. What if she don't like me?"

"Nobody is dancing with her right now, and I don't believe I've seen any other boys ask. It would be a shame if the prettiest girl you'd ever seen didn't get asked to dance because you were too nervous to ask her, now wouldn't it?"

Tommy agreed, and when the music started, he walked fearfully to where the girl of his fourteen-year-old dreams was sitting and muttered an invitation to dance. To his surprise, she accepted, and he nervously led her to the dance floor where she talked, and he seemed to be struck dumb. He looked toward Jim and was red with embarrassment clear to his ears.

A deal is a deal, and Jim headed toward Elizabeth to ask her for the next dance. He was surprised to see a handsome, smiling blond stranger leading her onto the floor. He was an excellent dancer, and Jim decided that he didn't like this stranger at all. He knew he was being childish, but he thought that he should be the one dancing with her, not some handsome stranger.

When the song ended, Jim walked to where the couple was standing.

"Oh, James, this is Bob. He's just passing through and heard about the dance. He decided to come in and join the fun before he went on his way. Bob, this is James Harding. He's my ranch foreman."

The musicians struck up a lively tune. Jim wanted to punch Bob right in the smiling lips, but he resisted the urge, shook his hand, and asked Elizabeth to dance instead. They whirled away from the outlaw leader, and Jim soon relaxed enough to enjoy the dance. He saw Tommy dancing with Denise and twirled Elizabeth up close to them. "I see that you survived. Did you tell her that you think she's the prettiest girl you've ever seen?" he teased.

"Yes, sir, I did." The boy beamed. "Did you tell Miss Davis that she's one of the prettiest girls you've ever seen?"

"Well, umm, not exactly." It seemed that his joke had backfired on him, and now it was his turn to be embarrassed.

"Only one of the prettiest, not *the* prettiest like Tommy told Denise?" She laughed. It had been a long time since she had danced, and she was enjoying herself. The night was young, and the flush on her face revealed the joy she was feeling at the moment.

As the night wore on, Jim and Elizabeth danced with each other and with several other partners. "Smiling Bob," as Jim dubbed him, made the rounds but didn't appear to be any more interested in Elizabeth than he was in anyone else. Even so, Jim kept an eye on him. He seemed too smooth, or maybe Jim was just a little jealous.

Jim had a feeling that he was being watched but had no idea why. His years of living on the range and hunting both wild game and men had given him almost a sixth sense that had saved his life on more than one occasion, so the feeling made him uneasy.

The truth was that Smiling Bob had several members of his gang keeping their eyes on Jim and making quiet inquiries to learn all they could about him. The outlaw leader knew that information on one's adversary was invaluable when involved in the things he was involved in. Strangers were welcome and plentiful at the barn dance, so trying to locate a watcher in the crowd would be a fruit-less endeavor. That was something that Smiling Bob was counting on. What he didn't count on was Jim's sense of unease when danger was near. Jim couldn't shake the feel-ing, even though he could not pinpoint its cause, and his senses were buzzing with the feeling of being watched by unfriendly eyes.

The night flew by with only a few minor altercations late in the night. The outlaws followed their leader's orders and stayed out of trouble and began to file out of town as the festivities began to wind down. Some of them carried sev-eral servings of liquor, but their fear of repercussions from Smiling Bob kept their usual affinity for trouble under con-trol even in their inebriated state. Such was his control over the assortment of villains and desperados.

Chapter 16

Early the following morning, the town began to recover from the effects of the previous night's festivities. The celebrants slowly began to wake from the late night and prepare for the Sunday morning church services and the afternoon box social. Families made breakfast around campfires near their wagons and buggies. The town seemed to rise in the same festive mood in which it had retired the night before.

The church services were festive with the message dwelling on friendship and delving into the story of David and Jonathan. The services were followed by a box social. Cowboys counted their cash and tried to find out which box lunch belonged to which girl before the bidding started. Every one of them hoped to have the winning bid for their favorite girl's picnic lunch. If so, they would get to spend a picnic lunch with the girl. If it was the wrong lunch, at least they got to have a picnic with one of the girls from the area. Unknown to Jim, Aunt Mable had persuaded Elizabeth to make up a box lunch for the auction. It was expected of all of the single ladies over sixteen to participate, and the single men were only too happy to spend their money for the chance to picnic with one of the many girls from the valley.

As the lunches were set up on a table for inspection by prospective bidders, Aunt Mable found Jim off to the side watching the preparations. "Too bad Dwayne won't make it today. I think there was a certain young lady who would have liked to have him bidding. Somehow I think she would have found a way for him to know which one to bid on. He has two months' pay coming too, so he probably could have afforded it," Jim said.

"Speaking of Dwayne, he did want me to ask you about maybe getting a little bit of his pay. He wants me to bid on a certain picnic basket in his name."

"Laid up like he is, he still found out which basket was Miss Cochran's? Of course I'll get him his pay before the bidding starts."

"That's fine. Now as for you, there is a certain blue basket with a large red bow that you *will* be bidding on. I'll point it out, but you had better bid on it."

Jim gave Aunt Mable a surprised look. He had not planned on participating at all unless some poor girl's basket didn't receive any bids. He had been to box socials before and had seen how hurt a girl could be if no one bid on her box lunch. He had enjoyed many a lunch and long conversation just making sure that no girl's efforts went unrewarded.

"Well, I really hadn't planned on it. I usually bid on a lunch if no one else does. I hate to see some girl disappointed by not selling her lunch basket."

"Fiddlesticks. Today you can bid on the one I show you. Besides, there isn't one basket around here that will go unsold."

"I don't think I need to ask who said basket belongs to, do I?"

"If you do, you're not half as smart as I gave you credit for."

The first basket up was a simple brown basket, and the bidding started low. A young cowhand from the C&O ranch got it for a dollar and collected the lunch and the young lady who prepared it. So it went with the bidding and good-natured teasing that went with this type of affair. Some of the cowhands purposely bid up the basket one of their friends was trying to bid on just to make things interesting.

A white wicker basket was brought to the block, and the bidding started quickly. Obviously, whoever made this basket was very popular, and her identity was known. When the basket hit the ten-dollar mark, Aunt Mable started bidding. Cheryl Cochran stood to the side beaming with pride that so much was being bid on her basket. It took fifteen dollars of Dwayne's hard-earned money to claim the prize. Before escorting Cheryl to the boardinghouse to have lunch with Dwayne, Aunt Mable pointed out which basket Jim was to bid on just in case she didn't get back in time.

A large basket with a red plaid cloth covering it came up, and only Dean Morrish seemed to be bidding on it. While not knowing whose it was, Jim still decided to bid it up on him just because nobody else seemed willing to. He made a glowering Dean spend eight dollars on the basket. Jim could see why he had gone that high on it when Olivia Olson came forward shyly as he stepped forward to pay.

The tall, raven-haired girl with big brown eyes was far from homely and exuded a certain inner strength.

"She deserved to have you bid a little more," Jim joked good-naturedly.

Dean looked ready to explode for a minute and then smiled in return. "Yeah, she did. Just remember though that what goes around comes around." Dean walked off with Olivia on his arm. He walked through his crew on the way to lunch. Turning, he waved at Jim before disappearing with his prize.

Several other baskets were auctioned off before the basket indicated to Jim came up to be bid on. Some of the young men who had as yet to secure a basket started bidding on the well-decorated container of food. When the bidding got to the two-dollar mark, Jim upped it to three and was surprised when a puncher from the Swinging M bid four dollars and another bid five. Jim bid six, and then the bidding war started. When Jim finally submitted the final bid at twenty-four dollars, he began to understand the wave and smile that Dean had sent his way. He had to laugh. *Serves me right,* he thought.

Jim paid the auctioneer and picked up the basket and was joined by Elizabeth, who blushed at how high her basket sold for. It was the highest price anyone could remember being paid for a box lunch in Lone Oak. The two walked away together to find a place to enjoy their picnic.

While they ate their lunch, Jim filled Elizabeth in on what he had been doing.

"I hope that you don't mind, but I've been making some inquiries and have sent for some help. We need to grow the herd some too, so I arranged a trade of some of the market-ready stock for some young breeding stock. They'll be here in the next couple of weeks. I know I might be overstepping my authority. Let me know if I am or if you want me to stop."

"I don't know how I can afford more hands. Otherwise I trust your decisions," she responded.

"Don't worry about their payroll. They owe me a favor or two, so you won't be on the hook for that. Maybe feeding them, but that's all. Now, what do we have for lunch?" He had purposely left out the fact that they were already his employees.

The rest of the picnic was spent enjoying the meal and small talk. Talk of hopes and dreams replaced the day-to-day talk of ranch work. Jim avoided talking about his family other than in generalities. He enjoyed being with Elizabeth, but the scars of his past were deep, and he did not want them opened for the world to see. They were still painful even after all of these years. That was all right because Elizabeth seemed more than happy to talk about the present and the future rather than the past. Jim talked of the wild lands that he had traveled, and Elizabeth listened intently while he spoke of them.

"The mountains to the north and west of here have some of the strangest things you could ever imagine. In the dead of winter, I've seen ponds so hot you could almost cook eggs in them and a mound that shoots streams of hot water and steam fifty feet in the air. There are waterfalls that drop two hundred feet into the bottom of a canyon, and the trout in the streams are as long as a man's arm. There are huge rams that battle for the ewes by crashing headlong into each other. Their massive, curled horns make so much noise when they collide that you can hear them from a mile away." His eyes shined at the memories of his travels through the Yellowstone Valley. He had gone there with Preacher, following a pack of wolves that had been killing stock in the area one fall. They had stayed through the winter hunting and trapping to meet their needs and to make a few extra dollars for their time in the valley.

"When spring finally arrived, the valley floor was covered in mountain laurel and buttercups. We stayed until late spring when the grizzlies started to become too numerous to ignore. By then we had watched dozens of moose and elk calve. As dangerous as a grizzly can be, watching the cubs waddling around behind their mothers and wrestling in the flower-filled meadows could make you smile—from a distance, of course. It's hard to believe that those little, clumsy balls of fur would grow into something as huge and ferocious as some of the old silvertips I've seen."

"It sounds magnificent. The most I travel in the wild is to the ranch and back. Perhaps someday."

Jim helped Elizabeth to her feet and picked up the basket. The two headed back to town. It was time for him to get back to work, and he wanted to visit Dwayne before heading back to the ranch. He had a feeling that something was coming and that he needed to be at the ranch.

"I'm going to check in on Dwayne and then Whitey, and I need to head back out to the ranch and get back to work. Two whole days without working is making me lazy."

They parted at the boardinghouse, and Jim went to gather Whitey and get back to the ranch.

The mood on the way back to the S Bar S was jovial. The festive mood from the fair carried over to the trip. Laughing and joking, the two men arrived at the ranch yard shortly after sundown. The place felt lonely and desolate after having Aunt Mable and Elizabeth at the ranch.

"Seems awful quiet," Whitey stated when they pulled up in front of the bunkhouse. The past weeks of having someone around accentuated how lonely ranch life could be. The dark windows and lack of smoke from the chimney was like a cloud raining down on a parade.

"A bit different than it has been. There's still plenty of work to do, just fewer distractions."

"What you planning to do until Thad makes up his mind? We still can't hunt rustlers and tend to the ranch by ourselves."

"We'll make a sweep up to the north and see what we can see in the morning. About midday we'll head to the Swinging M and see if there's an answer. Either way, we'll ride loose in the saddle and keep our eyes open and our powder dry. We'll have some more help in a couple of weeks, but we need to hold our own until then."

The men quickly dismounted and stripped the saddles from their mounts. They unloaded the wagon; and while Jim stowed the harness, Whitey headed to the bunkhouse to get a fire going to ward off the evening chill.

Chapter 17

Sunrise found the two men in the saddle and headed north to make a sweep of the range. As they swung southeast toward the Swinging M, they crossed the tracks of several riders heading into the rough breaks near the boundary of the Swinging M and the S Bar S. Dismounting for a closer investigation, Jim committed the different tracks to memory. Like fingerprints, the tracks of each horse were different and distinct. A good tracker could tell a great deal about the animals and their riders by studying the sign they left. Jim was a very good tracker and took his time now. If he saw any of these tracks again, he wanted to be sure he could recognize them.

All of the horses were shod, ruling out a passing band of Shoshone or Blackfoot. The eight sets of distinguishable tracks showed all of horses to be well fed and rested. The group was traveling at a relaxed pace and showed no signs of pursuit or concern about hiding their trail.

The band of riders seemed to be heading somewhere specific, but there was nothing in the direction they were heading. At least there was nothing that Whitey knew of in that direction, and he had been in the area since it had just begun to open up to white settlers.

"There ain't nothing up that way for a few days' ride. Some pretty country but no settlements or ranches. Should we see where they're going?"

"We can follow them a little way to see if we can learn anything. I don't want to take any chances though. There's too many of them for us to tackle if there's trouble. Maybe it's just some travelers from the fair in town." Jim doubted it, but it was possible. They were heading into no man's land, following a route they knew too well to be travelers unfamiliar with the area.

Turning to the northwest, the two followed the unknown riders for a mile or two, stopping several times to dismount and examine a few strands of hair or some droppings or some other clue that might help identify the riders or their mounts. As the trail came out on a large stone outcrop, it simply disappeared. Jim should have been able to find some scratches or scuffs on the rock surface to indicate what direction the riders went, but there was nothing. After the first few yards, the trail simply vanished.

"Strange. Eight riders couldn't cross even the hardest of cap rock and leave no trace, but I can't find anything. It's like they rode onto this rock and vanished, like they sprouted wings and flew off or the ground swallowed them. We don't have time to hunt for sign, but we'll come back later with help. For now, let's get to the Swinging M and talk to Thad."

Swinging back astride the gray gelding he was riding, Jim led the way toward the Swinging M. All the way to the Morrish ranch, he couldn't shake the feeling that he had missed something. It would have to wait until after they had finished their visit with Thad.

It was midafternoon when they rode into the ranch yard at a much more leisurely pace than the last time Jim had arrived. Thad met them as they pulled up in front of the cook shack.

"Climb down and join me for lunch. I figure you're here about our meeting in town."

When Whitey and Jim had dismounted and headed toward the open doorway, Thad turned to Jim and said, "I think I owe you something."

Jim didn't see the punch coming and was flattened by the hard right. Stars swam in his vision, and bells rang in his head. Thad smiled and bent to help him back to his feet. Shaking his head to clear the fog, Jim stared hard at the ranch owner, not quite sure what to think.

"You busted up two of my boys, hired away one of my best punchers, and whipped my boy, so I figure I owed you. I still think you came off light, but I'll call it even."

Jim knew the pride of Western men, so all he could do was take Thad at his word. He understood the need to keep face in front of his crew as well. "If my getting kicked in the head by a mule is what it took to make us even, I think we are. Man, can you punch." He was glad that it was the younger Morrish with whom he had fought and not the old man.

Whitey chuckled softly. "You should have seen that one coming."

The two followed Thad into the solid building. Jim got a better idea about the nature of this gruff rancher. The cook shack was built of heavy, closely fitted logs, and every possible gap was tightly chinked against the harsh Wyoming winters. The Spartan furnishings were well constructed and functional. The windows were set in the wall to make the best of the summer breezes to cool the kitchen and remove any smoke from the cook stove. Sunlight flooded the room, eliminating the need for candles or lamps during daylight hours. The fireplace had a huge brick oven built into it for the baking of bread and occasionally doughnuts or other delicacies for the ranch crew. A hand pump was installed along the rear wall near a large catch basin that drained out the back wall and away from the foundation of the building. If there was enough food, the building could be defended from attack for a long period of time without the need to leave for anything.

"Have a seat." Thad waved a hand toward the benches along the table. His cook brought a fresh pot of coffee and cups without a word and poured a cup for each man. Placing a bowl of sugar on the table for those who used it, he left the building so that the boss could talk in private.

"Frank says I should give you a listen. He seems to know you from somewhere and thinks you might be onto something."

"He's a good man." Jim didn't give any more information about how he and Frank knew each other. "I still think that the best way to fight the rustling is to band together. The rustlers are too well organized to take them on one ranch at a time. If we try that, they'll pick every ranch clean before they're through.

"What do you know about the land that lays to the north and west of the boundary between your place and the S Bar S?" Jim was fishing for information.

"Not much up that way. No settlements or towns but there's plenty of passes to the north from there. Tough country. Why?"

"Just wondering why riders would be going that direction."

"I couldn't tell you that," the rancher replied. His brow furrowed as he pondered Jim's response. "There ain't nothing up there but wilderness. Now about the Swinging M throwing in with the S Bar S, I was waiting for Miss Davis to get tired of ranch life and sell out. I kinda figured to buy her spread. Most everybody around knows it too. She has the best water and graze in the area and has no idea how to run a ranch. Just wanted you to know where I stand. I wouldn't run her off or anything, but I do want the S Bar S. The rustling may change that idea for now though."

"I appreciate you being honest, but I don't think she will be selling anytime soon. At least if I can help it, she won't be forced to sell. I'm glad to hear that you won't be trying to force her off her range. I ride for the brand, and I think you know enough about me to know I won't run. Besides, a range war would leave the whole valley open to rustling, and nobody wins in that kind of fight but the hired guns and the rustlers. Have you thought about what we discussed in town?"

"I've given it some thought, but I don't have hands to spare. I'll have Frank keep some riders working along the boundary between our spreads so they will be close to hand if needed, but I can't loan you any. I need what I got with branding coming up quick. It's the best I can do for now."

"I understand, and hopefully we won't need to call on them, but if we do, we might need to do it by signal instead of riding over and trying to find them. If we need help, I'll send up three smokes from our last location before we start tracking. We'll leave plenty of sign so it will be easy to follow from that spot forward. Is that all right with you?"

"That sounds like a workable plan to me. I'll pass the word to Frank, and he can start having some boys up along there by the end of the week."

The men rose, shook hands, and headed back out into the sunshine. Whitey and Jim mounted and headed back toward S Bar S range. Their pact with the Swinging M was all that they could ask for given the time of year and the work to be done on any ranch. His four extra hands would be here soon, he hoped—hopefully before the rustlers became bold enough to make a sweep of the valley and there was nothing left to defend.

Jim's thought process was interrupted. "He'll keep up his end of the bargain. He's hardheaded, but he's got enough pride to keep his word, no matter what it costs him. If he says there'll be men along the boundary by week's end with orders to help if called on, they'll be there. With anything resembling luck, we won't need them before then. It's the first I heard of him wanting to buy Miss Elizabeth out though. Don't surprise me none. What he said's true. She's got the best range around, and she ain't that knowing about ranching and cattle. I been trying to teacher her, and she learns quick, but there's plenty more for her to learn. Too much to learn in the time she's got. I reckon that's why you're here."

"Me?"

"Sure. I'm getting too old for this, and you know the business and won't run when things get tough. Maybe your wandering ain't so aimless as you think. I done what I can, but I can't be all she needs. I know more about you than you

141

might think. I know about the bad times and what Preacher done for you and what you done for him. He talked about you a good bit in his letters. They was long in between, but he wrote. One thing I will tell you though is don't you hurt that little girl. Tread light on her feelings. She's the reason I stuck around after Sam was killed. I'll kill the man that does her wrong."

Jim reined in sharply and stared in shock. "Wait a minute. Back up there. You knew Preacher?"

"Yeah, he was my younger brother. I appreciate what you done for him. He was right proud of you. His name was Daniel Jacob McKay, but everybody knowed him as Preacher. I reckon that's what he would have liked on his stone."

"He was a good man, Whitey. He didn't talk about any family though. As for hurting Miss Davis, I have no intention of doing wrong by her."

"Daniel and I didn't always see eye to eye on things, especially about God and such. I know how you two would ride into town and clean it up and ride out again. That was how he wanted me to be too, but that wasn't me.

"About Miss Elizabeth, I seen how she looks at you, boy, and if you ride out on her, she'll hurt something fierce. If you stay, it might hurt more. Do right by her. If you're gonna leave, don't lead her on. I'd hate to think evil of you."

Moving a couple dozen head of beef ahead of them, the two worked their way back toward the ranch. Jim had plenty to think about on the ride. Whitey had given him some information that he had never known. Preacher had a brother. No wonder Whitey reminded him so much of Preacher. They were more alike than Whitey knew.

The men left the small herd in a clearing near the ranch headquarters and rode into the yard just after dusk. Dark windows and stillness greeted them. There was no further discussion about Elizabeth, but Jim was sure that Whitey would take it personally if any man did wrong by her. He was glad to let it drop. Whitey probably thought of her as the daughter he had never had. Most of these old-timers had a soft spot for animals, children, lost causes, and damsels in distress, and Whitey was no different.

Chapter 18

It was a few days before the men returned to the area near the cap rock where they had lost the trail of mystery riders. The two dismounted and walked onto the hard surface, searching for any sign that might have been left. The rock might not accept marks of passing as easily as did sand or clay, but it also held them longer.

Whitey was the one who discovered a small bit of burlap stuck in a crevice of rock. That was what had failed to register with Jim the first time they had searched. He had used the same technique for disappearing himself before, only he had used buffalo hide rather than burlap. It left no trace while the burlap might fray, as some had obviously done this time.

"So that's how they did it. It's an old raiding trick. Your enemies follow you, and when you are ready to be rid of them, you ride onto a large rock outcropping, cover your horse's hooves with buffalo hide or something similar so they won't scuff the rock, change directions, and simply vanish. I've used it myself before. If the outcropping is big enough, it could be weeks before your pursuer even locates where you left it, if they ever do. I do believe that this is one of the trails the rustlers are using for themselves though, not to move cattle."

"What do you propose we do? Like you said, it could take weeks to find where they left the rock, if we ever do."

"We keep our eyes open and ride loose in the saddle. That bunch that Dwayne and I ran into was not worried about killing. I think that they were part of the same bunch that killed Sam. That only emboldened them. With him gone, the ranch was essentially fair game. That has changed now with two of us working the ranch and their spy gone. Killing one or both of us would open it back up. Once Dwayne is back on his feet and my boys arrive, Elizabeth should be able to make a go of this ranch."

"I've heard of some of your crew. If they're half as salty as the stories I hear, the rustling will stop soon enough. I heard that Flying Eagle feller could track a snake across a flat rock in a blizzard. Maybe he could work this trail out?"

"Don't tell him that, or he'll try to prove it. Besides, have you ever seen a snake crawl across a flat rock in a blizzard?"

Whitey smiled at how ridiculous the whole idea was. "Let's get back to work."

"We need to move some more marketable stuff in closer. I'm making a trade for some breeding stock from the Lazy H."

That night when they returned to the ranch, the ranch house was lighted, and the smell of cooking flooded the yard. Elizabeth walked out the door when she heard them riding in. Both men were surprised to see her there.

"Welcome back. I thought that you would be hungry, so I made you some dinner. Wash up and come on in."

Exchanging glances, the two men unsaddled and rubbed down their mounts before cleaning up to eat. A freshly cooked meal instead of the usual hurried evening meal would be a welcome change. They entered the dining room and saw the table covered with a colorful cloth, and oil lamps lighted the room as brightly as the midday sun. A small pot containing a bunch of wildflowers was sitting in the middle of the table. The men usually lit one lamp and never bothered with a tablecloth. Flowers were a woman's touch that never would have even crossed their minds.

"Dr. Halloran says that Dwayne will be able to travel safely soon. He thinks he'll be back in the saddle in another week or two as long as he doesn't push himself too hard."

Elizabeth had done her best to make the house welcoming. She wanted the men to feel at home when they arrived after a long day in the saddle. She had more than succeeded.

"Why are you here?" Jim asked. "I thought you were helping Aunt Mable and working for Joe."

She gave him a puzzled look. "Why shouldn't I be here? I do own the ranch, don't I?"

"Sure, but I thought you—"

"I'd shut up while I was ahead if I was you," Whitey interrupted. "That sure do smell good, Miss Elizabeth."

"As long as it isn't your cooking, Whitey, it will be an improvement."

"You two quit acting like children and sit down."

"She sure is one bossy boss lady." Whitey smiled.

Jim was smart enough not to continue that line of conversation.

Chapter 19

Bob had allowed the men to bring back whiskey along with the other supplies they had acquired in town. The camp was so far off the regular routes of travel that special trips had to be made for just about everything except meat. There was a ready supply of wild game in the area even for such a large group of men. Buffalo and elk made up a large portion of the protein in the men's diet. The whiskey was something that was allowed, because without it, several of the men would simply rebel and sneak it back into camp or leave. Rebellion was something he could not afford in a group such as this. Once it started, he would have to kill several of the mutineers or risk being killed himself. While it did not bother him to kill, there was the problem of replacing the dead members with new recruits. Most of the men were well into their cups when he called his lieutenants to his tent.

"That new foreman at the S Bar S is going to be trouble. He knew he was being watched the whole time. He could sense it. I could tell by the way he never was completely at ease. We need to get rid of him."

"That won't be so easy, boss," Keegan spoke up. "There's been plenty that's tried. Some say the Injuns call him 'Can't Die' or some such. I shot him myself before. Then he just shows up on your trail again. He wiped out the whole Jacobs Gang by his self."

"Maybe you just don't shoot so straight." Hunt was in a foul mood because he had been called away from his drinking. He was a mean drunk and was even worse when he was interrupted. He knew he couldn't take their leader in a gunfight, but Keegan might be a different matter. Besides that, the drinking had made him reckless, and he really didn't like the bug-eyed Keegan anyway.

Keegan stepped away from the table where the men had gathered. "If you think you can shoot straighter, just have at it." This was a chance that Keegan had been hoping for. Hunt was currently second in command, but if he were killed, Keegan figured he could step right into his shoes. If Hunt were sober, the two men might have been a close match, and Keegan would never try it that way, but Hunt had enough liquor in him to slow his reflexes and make him careless. It also made it easier to goad him into a fight. "Well, what're you waiting for?"

Hunt made a grab for the heavy Walker pistol on his hip. It was a move that was far slower than it would have been had he been sober. In his inebriated state, he imagined his movements to be smooth and flawless. They were not. The clumsy, drunken move had been anticipated by Keegan, and his Navy Colt cleared leather well ahead of his opponent. He calmly aimed and fired a single shot. Struck between the eyes by the .36-caliber ball, Hunt's head snapped back, and he crumpled into the dust.

"I guess you can shoot straight enough. He's your meat. You get him out of camp," Smiling Bob ordered. "Do it after we are done here, but drag him out of my sight for now."

Keegan was only too happy to comply. His number-one rival had been eliminated, and now he was second in command. After dragging Hunt's body from the tent, Keegan returned, and the meeting began.

"I already said it once that the new S Bar S foreman needs to be eliminated and or we need to make a clean sweep of the valley soon and then haul our freight."

"How, boss? Maybe Haskell could get a shot at him with that Sharps he's so proud of? He claims he was a Union sharpshooter during the war."

"A half dozen of us could ambush him up along the north tree lines. With rifles we could make short work of him."

A few other suggestions were made before Bob waved them all to silence. "You know him a bit, Keegan. What do you think?"

Keegan wet his lips before speaking. He was enjoying being the center of attention and smiled to himself. "I reckon that he'd sense an ambush. I don't know how he does it, but he slipped through many a trap we'd set for him in the past, and he'd do it here as well. Maybe it's the time he spent with them Cheyenne. I don't know. As for someone gunning him, I don't know anyone 'cept maybe the boss what's fast enough. He's greased lightning with them Colts of his. If Haskell can hit him from long range, that's our best bet. The longer the range, the better."

"You think he's that tough, do you?" The bandit leader grinned. "Get Haskell in here now, and we'll put him on it."

The man who was beckoned was a thin, ferret-faced man with no moral objections to killing long distance or shooting a man in the back. He was a man completely without scruples. To him, killing a man, woman, or child was no different than shooting a squirrel or a target. It just paid better. He wore dirty buckskins and had a scraggly red beard that matched the tangled mass on top of his head. His black eyes were like those of a weasel and displayed no emotion. What he lacked in social graces, he made up for in his wood lore and ability to call his shots out to eight hundred yards plus.

He arrived with his ever-present rifle under his arm and listened to what he was to do. "It'll cost an extra hundred. It'll maybe take me a couple weeks to do it, but it'll be done. Don't look for me until I get back. I'll bring you his scalp for proof that the job is done." That had always been Haskell's proof of completion, and his reputation was known through much of Wyoming and Montana. Without a backward glance, he departed, taking his few belongings with him.

"There we go now. That should eliminate a big thorn in our side," the outlaw leader said smugly.

Chapter 20

It was two weeks since the barn dance, and Dwayne had just returned to the ranch. The doctor had warned against riding more than a short distance or doing too much, but Dwayne felt the need to get back to work. Jim assigned him duties that kept him close to the headquarters and that would not overexert him. While Dwayne complained about being treated like a child, he pitched in and did what he was asked. At the end of each day, he was spent and thankful that he hadn't been expected to do his usual day's work, but his strength was returning.

The Lazy H herd had not yet arrived, so Whitey and Jim worked the range oftentimes by themselves. Jim had sent Whitey a few miles to the southwest to round up some cattle that had been spotted near the Cabot farm, and Jim wanted them pushed back before they decided to devour the produce or trample the fields. It was a short, easy trip, so Jim had Dwayne ride along with Whitey. The trail that had vanished along the cap rock had been bothering him since he and Whitey had discovered it, and he now took the time to investigate it further.

He knew Whitey would suspect something if he rode out wearing anything other than his usual attire and headed toward the Swinging M boundary. He had had the feeling of being watched for the past few days as well and knew better than to ignore it. He didn't want company for what he was planning. He worked better alone in these circumstances, with no distractions and only himself to watch out for. For that reason he rode off a short way from the ranch before circling back to make his change.

After watching Whitey and Dwayne ride out for the day, he made his way back to the bunkhouse and made his changes. He donned his buckskins and a nondescript gray felt hat. Smudging a little bit of soot from the chimney onto his face and the backs of his hands, he reduced the shine of his skin. Returning to his mount, he swung astride. The only things he retained from his normal clothing were his gun belt and his moccasins. Elizabeth came from the house just as he turned the steel dust mare to leave the yard a second time.

"Oh my, I barely recognized you!" she exclaimed. "What in the world are you doing dressed in such a fashion? You look like a wild man."

Jim had hoped to leave without being noticed, but it was too late for that now. "Hunting," was all he said. He smiled and rode off, hoping she wouldn't ask him what he was hunting for. Her puzzled gaze followed him as he headed off toward his destination. She noted that he was carrying his rifle rather than leaving it in the saddle scabbard but didn't give it any thought.

He rode at a steady trot until he was within a few miles of the lost trail. He slowed to a walk and dismounted when he was a half mile from the bare rocks. Worming his way through the brush for another hundred yards or more, he let his eyes drift over every inch of the area, looking for a clue as to why he had the feeling of being watched and impending danger. His life had been spared more than once because he had paid heed to the invisible warning bells. He would not ignore them now.

After more than an hour of studying possible ambush sites, Jim crawled back to his horse and mounted. The sense of danger was still strong, so he rode forward with great caution. His eyes took in every possible hiding spot for five hundred yards and registered anything that looked out of place. As he rode into the open, the hair on the back of his neck stood up, and he felt a knot in the pit of his stomach. Something was wrong, and the horse could sense the tenseness of her rider. Bending low over her neck to calm his mount, he heard the sinister *thwap* of a close, passing bullet and felt a slight tug on the back of his shirt. Had he not bent at just that moment, he would have been a dead man.

From the corner of his eye, he saw what he thought might be a slight puff of gun smoke nearly eight hundred yards away. Knowing anyone who could make that kind of shot with confidence would be unlikely to miss if given a second chance, Jim booted the mare in the ribs and sent her at a gallop toward some cover closer to where the hidden marksman lay in wait. Tumbling from his mount when she passed through some brush, Jim maintained his grip on his rifle and rolled into the undergrowth.

Now it was a waiting game. It was a game of cat and mouse, with the result being death for the loser.

The day grew hotter as the sun rose higher into the sky. Rivulets of sweat began to ooze from his pores as Jim lay silently where he had dropped from his mount. Salt from the sweat found the slight gash in his back caused by the bullet. When he rolled into the brush, some dust and leaves from the ground stuck to the wound, stopping the bleeding; but the salty sweat washed into the wound caused burning and stinging. Still, Jim lay motionless, ignoring everything but the area around where he thought the shot had come from.

The Cheyenne had stressed motionlessness when raiding or in this type of situation. Only his eyes moved, watching for any movement or indicator of human activity in the area. This was a time for patience. Many times the first to move was the first to die.

A large prairie rattler crawled toward Jim, flicking its forked tongue to determine exactly what this thing was on the ground in his territory. The snake shook its tail, giving the tell-tale buzzing sound that was its namesake. When rattling didn't move this prostrate creature before it, the snake crawled closer and gave its warning a second time. Jim continued the silent survey of his surroundings without moving. To move now would only earn him the strike of the snake. He had seen Cheyenne warriors lay motionless as more than one of these loathsome creatures crawled near or even over their bare legs or torsos. Eventually, the snake would realize that Jim was no danger to him and move along. Crawling under his right ankle and over his left calf, the snake did just that and was gone into the undergrowth.

The day was growing hotter, and thunderheads began to form in the west. The wind began to increase as the clouds grew, and shadows began to move swiftly over the ground.

Motion now would be difficult to detect. It had been almost an hour since the hidden marksman had fired, and Jim was beginning to wonder if the shooter had retreated when a crow that was about to land some six hundred yards away suddenly veered off and cawed raucously. The shooter had moved a few hundred feet from where the initial shot was fired without being detected by Jim's keen gaze. He was apparently very good at his trade.

The first spattering of rain began to fall as Jim finally detected a slight movement where the crow had changed course. A dull brown showed for a split second among the gray-green leaves of the sage brush. Jim now had his attacker pinpointed, and it was time for him to begin the very dangerous task of stalking his human target.

Inching ever so slowly to his left, he found a small crease in the stone and slipped silently into it. The fold in the ground traveled in the general direction he wanted to go, and by crawling, he could remain hidden from his hunter until much closer. While a good rifle shot himself, there was no way he could make the kind of shot required to end this confrontation at the same range as this hidden marksman.

Huge drops of rain began to fall as thunder rumbled to the west. The rain would help cover his movements, but it would also help hide the sound of any approaching enemy. As the rain increased, the small trench in which Jim had sought shelter from the gunman began to fill with runoff. Soon it would be untenable.

Jim had managed to inch his way along to a location where the brush would conceal him as he left the filling trench. Creeping slowly from the deepening water, Jim eyed the area where he had seen the tiny patch of brown, unable to detect any other movement.

The storm clouds blackened the sky, and lightning split the air. The rumble of thunder shook the ground. If the storm grew more intense or drew nearer, handling a rifle would become a very dangerous proposition. Any metal object could draw a lightning strike and prove fatal. The long barrel of a rifle had proven to be the death of more than one man. Even his hunter would be forced to abandon his weapon of choice in a fierce storm, and this one looked to be just that.

Blowing in from the northwest, the winds whipped at the low brush and made the rain fall almost horizontally. Lightning peeled across the sky; again the crack of thunder followed it almost immediately. Unless he wanted to become a lightning rod, it was time to abandon his rifle. His adversary would have to do the same or risk drawing a lightning strike himself. Jim slid his rifle away from himself into a place he would be able to retrieve it when the storm let up, assuming he survived to do so. He memorized the location and slid silently at an angle toward his enemy.

Watching intently where his intended victim had tumbled from his horse, Haskell looked for the tiniest of movements. He went through the reloading process without giving thought to it. He had done it so often that it required very little consideration on his part. He had missed, which was something he was not used to doing, and he planned to correct that mistake. He had been sure of his shot going where he intended it to go, but somehow the man he had fired upon moved unexpectedly just as he squeezed the trigger. If his target had moved a split second later, he would have been dead, but somehow the movement was timed just right, like an invisible hand had guided him.

There was no time to ponder this now. He had been given a job to do, and he intended to do just that. His dispassionate eyes scanned the deceptively flat-looking ground several hundred yards away. The buckskin attire worn by his adversary blended well with the surrounding landscape, and movement was the most likely thing to give away the location of his intended victim. Impatience was deadly in this situation, and Haskell was a patient man. He had hunted Indians who were less patient than he was and had collected the bounty on many a young bucks' scalps when they showed their impatience. Old warriors were far less likely to move, but the man he was hunting was a white man, and usually they were far less patient than even a young warrior out to prove himself and count coup.

Time dragged, and no movement was detected. After what he thought was an hour or close to it, Haskell began to wonder if his shot had been more deadly than he had initially thought. Even so, he would not make the mistake of going directly to where he had last seen his target. Instead, he edged to the west ever so slowly to get a better view of the ground before him. Thunderheads were beginning to gather, and he would need to finish this job quickly if he was going to do it with a rifle shot. Once the lightning got close, he may have to abandon his trusted weapon of choice, but he was confident he could finish the job with his blade or pistol if need be. No one had ever escaped him before, and there was no reason to believe that today would be the first time.

A crow changed its direction of flight just before landing overhead. He had thought he was invisible, but the sharp-eyed bird had seen him. Now he would need to move even more cautiously. Keeping his eyes on the location he thought Jim might be, he again moved slowly and silently. The wind picked up, and detecting movements was going to become very difficult at best. He needed find his quarry quickly if he wanted to avoid hunting a man in the deluge to come.

Moving stealthily at an angle that would bring him closer to the spot he thought Jim had fallen, Haskell scanned the area for movement. His keen eyes searched for anything that looked out of place or like it may have been disturbed. He was still too distant to make out details, but he could make out the broken brush where the rider had crashed to the ground. He pulled a small, collapsible telescope from his pouch and studied the area with greater detail than he could with the naked eye. Even so, the man who should have been killed by his bullet was nowhere to be seen. This wasn't going to be a simple kill. Even with the storm rolling in, he refused to abandon his long-barreled rifle. Maybe he'd keep it even when the storm rolled in.

Slipping silently in the general direction of his enemy, Jim scoured the area with keen eyes. The sky blackened as the thunderheads moved swiftly over the mountains. Lightning split the sky, and thunder crashed, shaking the very ground under foot. The blackness of the storm was illuminated once again by a discharge of static electricity. In the brief brightness, Jim spotted his hunter once again trying to slip closer to where he would have fallen if the bullet had struck its mark, or, more accurately, if the target had not moved at the last second. Jim once again gave a silent prayer of thanks and began his stalk. The hunter had become the hunted.

Jim's mind sought the possible name of his ambusher. Very few men could make that kind of shot. He dismissed the names one by one as he crept ever closer to the man who had tried to kill him. Knowing who his enemy was would aid in his hunt. His father and the Preacher had both taught him that if you can figure out who your adversary is, you can figure out what his tactics are and be one step ahead of him.

The war between the states had produced many men who could make long-range shots, but most of them had faded away without ever using the specialty rifles they had used during the dark period in the nation's recent history. Most hated the thought of what war had forced them to do, but some had taken a liking to long-range killing. Their lack of a conscience and natural hand-eye coordination made them efficient killers. They seemed to derive pleasure and satisfaction by taking the life of other human beings. They killed for the sake of killing, like a weasel. These men were deadly, and their names were the ones spoken of and feared by those in wild places.

As he ticked off the names as dead, imprisoned, or known to be elsewhere, his thoughts came to rest on the name Haskell. A skilled rifleman with no reservations about killing from ambush, he was a notable woodsman. He was also a scalp-taker, literally. Knowing the probable name of his attacker stiffened Jim's resolve to eliminate him and send him to his just reward. How many he had killed was purely speculation, but the known number was in the dozens. Men, women, and children were all the same to him. As long as money was paid, the deed was done, and then he would slip off into obscurity to strike again somewhere else.

One disadvantage Haskell had was his weapon of choice was cumbersome, and he rarely used another. He was also extremely confident of his ability and never doubted his victims would be the ones who died. Jim planned to use that information. Even so, stalking a man like the one he now hunted was a dangerous undertaking, and Jim moved forward cautiously. He had to get to Haskell soon though, or the mare he was riding might return to the ranch and bring Whitey, unknowingly, into his sights.

Inching forward, Jim moved to within a hundred yards of the greasy-haired sharpshooter. On catlike feet he cut that distance by half and then half again. Haskell was so intent on the ground before him that he never heard Jim's soft approach. At ten yards Jim stopped. Haskell was on the opposite side of a very small opening in the brush. Even knowing the kind of man before him, Jim could not bring himself to shoot him in the back, so he cleared his throat and asked, "Are you looking for someone?"

Haskell spun with amazing speed and fired at where he had heard Jim's voice. Jim had wisely taken a step to his left and fired in return. Haskell missed. Jim didn't. Haskell's breastbone was shattered, and his lifeless body was flung into the mud with his sightless eyes staring up into the rain. Stepping forward, Jim retrieved the long-barreled Sharps and smashed the stock against a hard rock, shattering it and bending the barrel beyond repair. The rifle was a superb weapon, but it had taken so many lives that Jim could not bring himself to leave it intact. He then set out to find Haskell's horse. Leaving it where it was would make it easy prey for a passing predator or would cause it to wind up starving to death. Neither was acceptable to Jim.

He found the animal pulling against its restraints, but they held tight. Calming the animal, he loosed it and led it back to Haskell's body. A bit of the old, blackened heart of his and the thought of the irony mixed together to lead him to return a slight portion of Haskell and a message to whoever had hired him. Grabbing a handful of the tangled locks, Jim drew his skinning knife and made the quick cut necessary to remove the topknot. Taking the busted stock of the Sharps, he carved two words into it and tied it and the bloody scalp to the pommel of Haskell's horse before giving it a slap on the rump, sending it off into the wilderness. Like most horses, it would return to the place it considered home which, for this horse, would be the outlaw hideout. Jim knew he wouldn't be able to follow the horse, so he didn't even try. The mare he had ridden out this morning had already headed back to the home ranch and, by now, since she carried no rider, had probably already arrived home.

The storm had subsided almost as suddenly as it had arisen, so Jim retrieved his rifle from where he had left it and started the long walk back to the ranch. He hadn't traveled more than a few miles when he spotted a small group of riders coming his way from the direction he was heading. Recognizing two of the horses, he increased his pace slightly and headed toward the advancing horsemen. When he was near enough to identify the riders, he gave a shout and waved his arms overhead to get their attention. They spotted him and changed course slightly to meet him. Whitey was riding one of the ranch horses that Jim had recognized and was leading Buck, figuring Jim would need a horse when they found him.

As they rode closer, Jim recognized the rest of the riders. Skipper and Flying Eagle were riding with Whitey along with a rider from the Swinging M. He couldn't recall the fourth rider's name but that he was sent by Thad Morrish was a good sign. He found a handy rock and sat down to await the arrival of the group.

"Hi'ya, boss. I thought you knowed enough to come in out of the rain but just goes to show what I know. And then you sends that poor, frightened critter back to the ranch by her lonesome. You must be slipping up. Why, Whitey dang near burst a blood vessel worrying about that little mare." Skipper laughed merrily at finding his boss alive and well. An unseated rider in the mountains in a bad storm usually meant disaster, so his concern was warranted, and his relief was evident.

"Hi, Skip. When did you all arrive?"

"We blowed in just afore the storm hit. Whitey and that Dwayne feller met us as we was coming in and led us back to the ranch. Then that little mare come scooting in as the storm cut loose. She must've been running ahead of it the whole way in. She was plumb tuckered and spooked."

"There's a little lady at the house that's pretty near beside herself with worry. You better mount up, and we better head back before she calls out the cavalry. I reckon you'll give us details if'n you want on the ride." Whitey's face showed its relief, but he was a bit more sober-minded than Skipper. Flying Eagle was impassive as always, but he missed nothing.

"You're right about that. Let's get moving."

Swinging astride, Buck, Jim, and the other men headed back to the house.

"Miss Lizbeth told us you came back, changed, and went hunting when we got to the ranch. When the mare come back without you, I figured out where you headed. You mind telling me what you was thinking? That little girl is worrying herself sick."

"Well I was hunting. I just never told Miss Davis *what* I was hunting. I thought I might find a bit of a trail and find out where it led but didn't want to drag you along. Besides, I work better alone at things like this."

They rode in silence for about ten minutes before Jim spoke again. "I'm glad I didn't have you along this time, Whitey." He spoke very seriously. "It would have given Haskell another target, and I couldn't have lived with it if he had killed you, my friend."

"Haskell? He's around? We better ride sharp."

Flying Eagle spoke for the first time. "He doesn't miss, Jim." Full-blooded Sioux, Flying Eagle had nonetheless been educated in a Christian school and spoke fluent English. Even so he had retained much of his heritage as far as tracking, hunting, and stoic demeanor. If he had something to say, he would say it and let the chips fall where they may. If he didn't have anything productive to say, he said nothing.

"He missed twice today. He won't miss again." The meaning of the words didn't go unnoticed by the men he rode with. Even Flying Eagle's normally impassive face cracked a rare grin as he thought about his boss ending the life of such an evil man.

"Good."

"He didn't work for free though, so his boss is still around."

On the ride back, Skipper filled Jim in on the trail drive. "We didn't have no trouble coming down with eight of us, but we did hear 'bout a mixed herd that was being sold cheap at one of the mine settlements. Didn't have no time to check it out though. Josh probably might if he was of a notion. You should wire him and see."

"He's already keeping an eye out for that type of activity. He'll let me know of any new developments."

"Well anyways, we brought about thirty two-year-old bulls and the rest heifers. Josh told us to bring good stock, so we did. There was a well-used trail on the way down here though. Looked like someone'd been pushing stock to the north."

The Swinging M hand had remained silent until now. "You fellas come down from the north? There ain't no ranches up that way. Where do ya reckon the stock that was getting pushed your way come from? Did anyone mention the brands on that mixed herd?"

"They came from around here," Flying Eagle responded. "The trail they were using disappeared about twenty-five miles north of here. I couldn't tell you the brands, Patrick, but my guess would be they came from this valley."

"Nobody's shipped anything from hereabouts."

"You're right about that, Pat. Makes a man wonder, huh? Boss, you done good ridding this country of the likes of Haskell," Whitey commented. "That'd sure do a man proud to be the one to put that snake under."

"I'm not proud of what I did, Whitey, but it needed to be done. He would have bided his time and picked us off one by one. I'd appreciate it if nobody mentioned it to Elizabeth. I kinda sent a message back to his former employer. I don't like scalp-takers, so I was more of a scalp-sender, if you understand what I'm saying. Nothing to be proud of there."

"We'll keep mum, boss. You know us. Just feed us, and we'll be too busy eatin' to talk. So you sent his scalp back to his boss, huh? That for sure'd send a message, all right." Skipper laughed heartily at the ironic twist.

"You scalped him?" the Swinging M hand yelped. "That's…" He couldn't put together his thoughts to finish the sentence.

"Oh, be quiet, Thompson," Whitey growled. "Haskell was a scalp hunter, and it's only fittin' he got his topknot lifted while trying to lift an honest man's hair."

Jim turned the talk to the herd to be shipped and when they would be ready to move.

"We got about a hundred and fifty head ready to go, so they can head back north soon as you're ready for them to leave. Them four fellas you got to push them back to Montana look pretty able to handle the drive."

"They had better be. Even so, I think we'll give them a day or so to rest before we send them back up north."

Small talk filled the rest of the ride back to the ranch. As the group swung down from the saddle, the door to the house burst open, and a tanned and freckled redhead flew across the yard. Seeing that everyone had returned riding heads up and toes down, Elizabeth unashamedly threw her arms around Jim.

"You're all right, aren't you? I was so afraid when your horse came back without you. And then the storm, and…and…" Her voice trailed off, and she took the time to realize how she was behaving in front of a group. She stepped back a half step and looked around at the men. Taking a closer look at Jim, she noticed his muddy clothes and the slight bloodstain on his shirt.

"Oh, Jim." She gasped. "You're hurt and all muddy and probably soaked to the skin from the storm. You must be freezing and hungry. Come inside, and I'll fix you up."

Skipper couldn't help himself and snickered at his boss being fretted over in such a fashion.

"Can it, Skip," Jim growled.

"What is so funny, you ruffian?" Elizabeth chided. "You bring him back and probably never even thought to give him something to eat or to tend to his injury, or to make sure he wasn't cold."

Even Flying Eagle chortled at Skipper's reproof.

"Well, ma'am, I was just, umm, err..." For once, the gregarious Skipper was at a loss for words.

"And the rest of you go on now. Do something productive. Laughing at this poor man's injuries, you should be ashamed of yourselves."

Jim looked confused and shrugged his shoulders. All he could do was follow the worried young woman into the house. Nobody made that much fuss over him being out in the weather since his mother had been killed.

Once inside, she turned to him again. "Oh, Jim, I was so worried. When I told Whitey you went hunting, he got very serious. When your horse came back without you, I told the men to drop everything and go find you. Whitey said you were fine, but I could tell from his voice he was scared, and he doesn't get scared very easily. Now, here you are all muddy and bloody, and who knows how badly hurt you are." Her voice cracked slightly as she spoke.

"Elizabeth, I've hurt myself worse than this while shaving. I just got a bit of a scratch that barely even bled. It'll itch a bit for a few days, but it's not anything for you to get worked up about."

"Nothing for me to worry about! What do you mean?" Her face grew as red as her hair as her emotions rose to the surface. "You could have been killed or laying hurt like Dwayne was, and you tell me it's nothing to get worked up about! If you hadn't come back, I don't know what I would have done. Don't you tell me to not get worked up! Now take off that shirt so *I* can see how bad you are hurt!"

"I tell you it's nothing, and I'm not taking off my shirt, but I wouldn't mind something to eat."

"How can you think about eating right now? Now take that shirt off, or do I have to take it off for you?"

The Lazy H hands would have gone into shock if they had seen their unflappable boss subdued so easily by a woman. Obediently, Jim stripped off his shirt and turned his back to Elizabeth. The slight gash was nearly hidden among the older scars and had scabbed over. Seeing the scars, Elizabeth let out a slight gasp before ordering Jim to sit down on one of the wooden chairs in the kitchen so she could bandage his wound.

Clinching her teeth, she bathed the slightly puckered welt. The dust had sealed it against blood loss but had caused the injury to become somewhat inflamed. The gentle cleaning only took a few minutes. During that time, she studied the old wounds and wondered to herself how they had been inflicted and how they had helped form the man who was before her now.

"There now. You should be good as new in a short time."

Jim started to slip his shirt back on, but Elizabeth stopped him. "You wait just a minute, and I'll sew that up for you. You can't be going around with a rip in your shirt. It wouldn't be proper." She seemed to miss the incongruity of a ripped shirt being improper but a shirtless man in her house was not.

A few minutes later, she returned his shirt with the minor repair made. He quickly donned the repaired garment and started for the door. He had been doing a lot of thinking on the ride back to the ranch. Emotions and common sense seemed to be at war in his head. His brow puckered. Turning at the door, he spoke, "I have some things I'd like to talk to you about privately. Would you mind if we went for a walk later so we can talk?"

"Sure. I don't have any other plans right now." She smiled at him, adding to his uncertainty. "Dinner will be in an hour or so. We can talk after that."

"That will work," he responded before walking out the door.

Chapter 21

"He's been gone over two weeks," Smiling Bob growled. "How hard can it be to shoot a man?" The question was flung at his new lieutenant.

No word had been heard from Haskell since he had rode out to kill the new ranch foreman of the S Bar S ranch, and Bob was not a patient man. The torrential downpour that had soaked the valley they were hidden in four days earlier had done nothing to improve his disposition.

"I'm telling you, boss, that Jim fella ain't an easy kill. Haskell will get the job done though." Keegan was only too glad it was Haskell hunting Jim and not the other way around, as it had been almost ten years ago when Keegan and the rest of the Jacobs Gang were the prey. He knew all too well how relentless the target of his leader's wrath could be.

"Any man can be killed! All it takes is one well-placed bullet!" For once he wasn't smiling. "If he fails, we'll sweep the valley, take everything, and kill *anyone* who tries to stop us. I'm tired of this piecemeal way of rustling anyway. I want to sleep in a real bed under a real roof before the snow starts to fly."

A commotion at the edge of camp drew the attention of the two outlaws. A weary, riderless bay gelding was wandering into the camp. Two of the lookouts quickly rounded him up and were leading him toward where Smiling Bob was standing. Their faces showed uncertainty as they approached.

"I think it's Haskell's bay," one of the two men leading the horse muttered. He knew for a fact whose horse it was but dared not admit it. To acknowledge that someone of Haskell's reputation had failed made both sentries nervous. Bearing such news to their current boss was something neither one wanted to do.

"You *think*? You could have fooled me." The response was a snarl. "You know that horse as well as I do. Probably better. Bring it over here."

The gulp elicited from the one holding the horse was audible. The entire camp was growing restless over Haskell not returning, and now his horse had returned without him. Nobody was sure what the ringleader's reaction would be, and all were sure they did not want to be around to see it. Unfortunately, these two were the ones on watch when the horse wandered back to camp. They had seen the scalp and the shattered stock of the rifle. While neither one could read, both had an idea as to what might be carved into the hunk of hickory that had formerly been the stock of a long-range rifle. There was no mistaking what the hunk of hair and dried skin meant. Haskell had missed. The tangled mat of greasy red hair could only belong to one person.

"He missed?" Smiling Bob read the words carved into the wood. "How arrogant of him to send this back! I'll kill him for this. He dares to send *me* this kind of warning? Just who does he think he's dealing with?" The words were spat out like liquid venom. "We'll ride in four days and rid the world of that arrogant snob and take everything in that valley we want with us."

A plan was already beginning to formulate in the back of his mind. They would clear Lone Oak of every head of cattle it held and either kill this interloper in the process or see that he was in some way blamed. Nobody spoiled his plans and lived to tell about it—not United States Marshals, Texas Rangers, local sheriffs, and certainly not this meddlesome Jim character.

By the time night fell, the entire camp knew that Haskell had been killed and that their boss was in a foul mood. They had also heard of his bold plan to strip Lone Oak and ride out. To some that sounded like their big break. To others it sounded like Smiling Bob had finally lost his mind. There were far too many ranchers and ranch hands for them to handle and manage the rustled stock as well. Add to that the fact that this stranger they had heard of had killed Haskell, and some were ready to hunt for greener pastures. That night, some took advantage of the cover of darkness and slipped out of camp. Morning found six fewer outlaws in the camp, including the two lookouts who had first found Haskell's horse.

"Keegan!" The roar could be heard over most of the camp. "Keegan! What's going on? Where are those two that brought in Haskell's horse? Where are you, you worthless turd?"

"I'm right here, boss. What's all the shouting about? Them two was on duty last night and should be camped down by the chow tent."

"They're not there. Don't you think I know where they are *supposed* to be, you idiot? I wouldn't be asking if they were there. Now where are they?"

"I...I ain't for sure, boss, but I'll find out."

"You bet you will, and you'll do it quick."

"Yes, sir," Keegan spluttered.

Scouring the camp, Keegan discovered that there were four other men missing as well. He knew that this news would not sit well with their leader and tried to think of how to soften the blow but could not.

"Keegan, I see that we had a few leave us last night. Some of the boys was wondering what had them so spooked, and we figured it must be that new fella on that S Bar S ranch. He done for Haskell, didn't he?"

"Yeah, I reckon he did. Why?"

"A couple of them boys was pretty handy, so we figure if they pulled up stakes, we would too. You want to come with us?"

"Have you told the boss you're quitting him just before he makes the big haul?"

"Nope. We figured we'd do that on the way out of camp. Figured to take what he's been holding in his personal stash of cash along with us."

"Well why don't you come along and tell him yourself, Jones? I'm sure he'd be real receptive to your idea."

The leader of the mutineers snickered. "Lead on."

Keegan was thinking fast. He knew better than to cross Smiling Bob, but if he could deflect his anger toward Jones, he could avoid drawing attention to his own failure to keep tabs on the men. Leading the small group of rebels to the tent of their leader, he stopped and stepped to the right.

"Boss, them two that brought in Haskell's horse left camp. They pulled up stakes and lit out. They wasn't alone neither. It seems that there were four others that lit a shuck too."

The reply came through gritted teeth. "And what are you going to do about it?"

"Well, boss, it seems Jones here thinks it's a good idea to leave too, and he has something he wants to tell you."

"Why you, Keegan!" Jones realized too late he had been set up by the second in command. Keegan had quietly drawn his weapon upon entering the tent. Jones spun to face Keegan and was greeted by a bullet in the gut and another in the chest. He died without even reaching for his gun. The rest of the mutineers were caught completely unprepared.

"So do the rest of you feel the same way?" Smiling Bob had his gun drawn and was facing the small group at the entrance of his tent. "If you do, you are welcome to leave the same way Jones did."

"Uhhh no, boss. I think we changed our mind. We just wanted to offer our help on the last haul," one of the insurrectionists mouthed the words quietly. Their plan to ride out had been thwarted, and they now had two choices: go along with the planned raid in earnest or meet the same fate as Jones. Maybe the raid would pan out in the end anyway, so why not ride along?

"Glad to have your undying loyalty. Just don't forget who got you this far. Now get rid of that carcass before it starts stinking up the place. Tell anyone else who wants to leave that they can come ask me real nice like Jones did. I'm sure he'll like the company."

Chapter 22

After the dinner dishes were finished, Jim and Elizabeth walked quietly to a small creek just a few hundred yards from the house. The sun was sinking in the west as Jim took Elizabeth's hand.

"I have some things I need to tell you," he said softly. "Not all of them are good. As a matter of fact, most of them are pretty bad, but you need to know."

"Oh, Jim, what could possibly be so bad? We have some fresh stock, thanks to you. Dwayne is on the mend, and Whitey says we are in better shape than we've been in a long time. What could possibly be wrong?"

"Me." Jim's one-word answer drew only a quizzical look from the woman by his side. "I'm what is wrong. There is too much past that comes to the surface too easily. Too much blood. Too many battles."

"But, Jim, you never look for a fight. You're a good man. What are you saying? I don't understand."

He kicked the dirt with the toe of his boot. "No, I'm just a man and not always a very good one. I have killed men before—some without any remorse and others because they stood in the way of what I wanted to do. Always within the bounds of the law, but…" He couldn't bring himself to look her in the eye. He had only this day realized how fond he had become to her, and he knew that his past would follow him no matter where he went.

"Jim, that was the past. What are you saying? What's wrong? Is that where those scars came from?"

"No, it's not the past!" His response was harsher than he intended. "I went out today hunting for the rustlers. I knew when I left it would be dangerous and that I might have to kill again, but I went anyway. There wasn't anyone else that could go or that I would ask to go even if there was. And then when I get back, you make all that fuss over me because of what I had done. I killed a man today! True, he tried to kill me first, but I knew what I was hunting when I left."

"You mean that was a bullet wound? I thought you had been thrown and…oh, Jim, you could have been killed."

"But I wasn't, and another man died at my hand." His face contorted as he tried to bring his thoughts and emotions under control. How could he have been so stupid? He had dropped his guard in the one thing he knew nothing about, and now he was lost. Whitey had warned him about her feelings, and now… A groan escaped his lips as he sought the words to say. What he wanted to say was "I'm in love with you," but what he felt he needed to say was he had to go. How could he ask her to share his hurts and pains?

"Thank God you weren't killed." Her words disrupted his thoughts. "I couldn't have taken it if it had been you who was killed."

She wrapped her arms around his chest and wept. He took her tenderly in his arms and let her tears soak his shirt. He was even more lost than when he had started talking. His feelings sprang to the surface as her tears subsided. He turned her chin upward and kissed her gently and tenderly at first and then more fiercely as the passion they both felt threatened to ignite into a raging fire.

"No!" he almost shouted as he tore himself from their embrace. "No, it's all wrong. I can't—I mean, we can't. It's just not right. I wanted to tell you tonight that I have to leave the ranch. I'm getting too close. I can't let this happen."

"What do you mean *you* can't let this happen? Aren't there two of us? Don't I get a say in this matter? Don't I count? Who are you that you think you can play with my feelings and then decide *no* on your own?" The tears had begun again, but this time they were tears of pain and frustration.

"I'm sorry, Elizabeth. You saw the scars." His voice softened again. "I was a killer. I'm James Harding. Doesn't that name mean anything? Haven't you heard it before? I can't ask you to have feelings for me. I don't deserve it. I'll wrap things up so that your ranch will be safe and so you can keep it, but I can't stay myself. I'll be close by until things are sorted out, but then I have to leave. Don't you see? Everyone I loved has been killed. My father, my mother, Preacher, and my sister are all dead. All murdered. If Whitey had followed me sooner today, he would have been killed too. Don't you see?"

"No! I don't see. I don't care about the ranch. I never thought I could have feelings again after…after…"—she faltered slightly—"after Samuel died. Now I think I could, and you tell me no, not because you don't care but because you do. That doesn't make sense."

She began to weep again.

"It does when you know the whole story. When I was just seventeen, my family was slaughtered by a gang of outlaws. My father had fired the leader of the gang when he caught him stealing. He decided to come back and try to rob my father at gunpoint. Dad never took to being robbed. I don't know for sure how the shooting started, but my father and mother were dead by the time I got back to the ranch yard. Dad took some company with him when he went. I was shot and knocked unconscious. I came to just in time to see my little sister ridden down like a dog in the street. I knew before then that there was evil in the world, but even though father was a Montana ranger, I never knew how evil it was until that day.

"I learned to hate that day. I won't give you all the details, but I did get many of the scars I carry that day at the hands of those responsible for the slaughter of my family. Like I said, I learned to hate that day, and I hunted down all but two of those responsible for my family's murders. I killed all of them plus more."

"You don't have to tell me. It's the past. You're not that man anymore."

"No, I'm not him, but that old nature still comes out. I've killed too many to count. How can I even think that someone should care about me? I have done so much evil, and even though I know God has forgiven me, it has still shaped me into a man who can hurt another or take a life if need be. How can I expect you or any other woman to have feelings for a man like that?" His voice grew husky as he told the story he had never shared before with anyone but Preacher.

"You deserve the truth." Without embellishment or flare, he told the story as simply and honestly as he could. He left nothing out, including his meeting of Preacher and his accepting of Christ as Savior. When he finished, Elizabeth took his hands in hers. She wanted to take away all the pain but didn't know how.

"Oh, Jim, I'm so sorry you went through so much pain and loss, but that doesn't mean that is all there is for you. I don't believe God wants you to be alone all your life because of what some cowards did years ago or even because you lost your way. He brought you back to Himself for something. I just know it."

"I still don't know what that something is, and until I do, I can't ask anyone to share my journey. I will leave Whitey in charge. The boys who are here work for me, and they'll follow his instructions to the letter. You're in good hands. I'll be gone by tomorrow but not too far until the rustling has been stopped. I can't stay here. You see, Elizabeth, I did something I promised myself I would never do. I fell in love with you. Now I have to go. You see, I can't stay. I would be too close to you, and I couldn't take being that close without there being a future."

"That's it, isn't it? You're scared. You're afraid to get close because you might get hurt. Well that's part of life. You can't run away. That only hurts you more." Her face flushed as she confronted him. "I never thought you were a coward." The word *coward* cut like a knife. "I—"

"I'm a realist, not a coward! A coward would take the easy road, which would be to stay here with you, but you can't see that."

"You're right—I can't see that! Allowing yourself to have feelings takes guts. You're running from them." Elizabeth turned from him and ran toward the house with her hands over her face. He had done what he had hoped to avoid doing and had hurt her deeply. He walked farther into the growing dusk to a secluded area where he knelt and sought the Father's face.

"God, how come I let myself get so close? Why didn't I see what was happening? Why did I let her so close? I hurt her when I was trying to protect her."

Chapter 23

The next hour or so was spent in deep prayer as Jim wrestled with himself and his desires. He knew that part of what she had said to him was true. He was scared to allow himself to grow close to anyone again. What she had awakened in him, he had thought was long ago dead and buried. He had never permitted himself to care too deeply for anyone since Preacher had been killed. He had made friends but had shielded himself from that closeness of a true friendship, let alone love. Now that feeling was growing, and he was scared to let it take root too deeply.

It was well after dark when he returned to the bunkhouse. He looked at nobody but slowly began to pack. Even the talkative Skipper was silenced by his boss's brooding countenance. The eerie quiet seemed almost palpable as Jim thoughtfully packed his belongings. The men knew he had spoken to Elizabeth and expected him to be jovial when he returned instead of the morose man that was in their midst.

"In case you couldn't figure it out, I'm leaving. I want you men to follow Whitey's orders as if they were my own.

Whitey, you're the ramrod now. You know what needs done better than I do, so see that these guys earn their keep. I'll be around, but don't look for me here."

"What's eating you? You just up and quitting on her when she needs you the most?" Whitey's face contorted and began to turn red. "I thought you had sand!"

"You told me not to get involved with her! You know the kind of man I am, and you know I'm not one to run, but I have to leave!"

Whitey followed him as he left the bunkhouse. "You got too close, didn't ya, boy?"

Jim wheeled on him.

"Yeah, I'm an old coot, so I can still call you a boy! And I got two eyes that still see pretty good. You let yourself get too close, so now you're pulling up stakes."

"I said I wouldn't be far, and I'll make sure she's safe before I leave the country, but you called it right. I'm a no-account with nothing permanent to offer her."

"'No-account'! I heard about your operation up Montana way and know you could buy out this whole valley without even giving it a thought. She ain't never heard of the Lazy H, but I sure have. You got thousands of acres full of cattle, mines, and some of the best horseflesh north of Denver. What you are is scared of that little girl who thinks the sun rises and sets on your say-so."

"So what if I am? I'm still leaving."

"Have it your way then. I'll see she's cared for as best I can and that her ranch remains hers as long as she wants it so. Best of luck to ya."

Jim tightened the cinch and swung astride Buck. "It's for the best, Whitey. I know you'll look after her as if she was your own daughter, so I know she's in good hands." A despondent James Harding rode out of the ranch without a backward glance.

Elizabeth heard his horse trotting out of the yard and came running from the house. Tears streamed down her face as she watched his silhouette disappear into the darkness.

"The last words I said to him were in anger. I didn't even tell him good-bye properly. Now he's gone. I'll probably never see him again." She wept openly. Whitey muttered something unintelligible that brought no comfort. Dwayne and a couple of the Lazy H hands had come out and watched too as Jim rode away.

"What's he leaving for?" Dwayne demanded. "Don't he know he's needed here? I never figured him to run out on us."

"It ain't us he's running out on. He's skeered of something he don't know nothing about." Whitey said the words quietly, almost to himself.

"Me? He's scared of me?" Elizabeth had overheard the quietly spoken words.

"Miss Elizabeth, that man ain't scared of no man, but he don't know nothing about you female types. Fact being no man does, but he's let his guard down near you, and now he don't know what to do."

"Men! Why are you all so confusing? If he cares so much, he should just say so and stay, but he has to run. I just don't understand!" She whirled and headed back to the house. "To blazes with him! He's a no-account saddle bum anyway!"

Skipper whistled softly. "I reckon he got her some riled. I gotta stick up for the boss, though. He may be a no-account, but he sure ain't a saddle bum."

Whitey cleared his throat. "Well we got plenty to do and need to get started early, so let's turn in. No need to stand here gawking at the shadows."

The men returned to the bunkhouse. He himself awkwardly approached the silent house. Jim had gotten one thing right, and that was that Whitey would look after Elizabeth as if she were his own daughter. He knocked softly.

"Miss 'Lizabeth? It's me, Whitey. Mind if'n I come in for a minute?"

"Come on in, Whitey." She sniffed. "Please tell me you're not quitting too."

"No, ma'am," he replied after entering the house and closing the door behind him. "I don't reckon I'm gonna do that. I'm too old, stubborn, and comfortable here to even think such a thing."

"Why did he go? What did he mean when he said, 'I'm James Harding. Doesn't that name mean anything to you?' He's just Jim to me. He said he was a killer, but I don't see that."

"Did he tell you about his family? About living with the Cheyenne? Or how he set out when he was just nineteen to kill a bunch of men? Those was what he was talking about. I wanted to let you know the boys and me will make a go of the ranch for you. I'll stay on as long as you'll let me, and while I ain't Mr. Harding, I do know a little about cows."

"Thank you, Whitey. I don't know what I would do without you. You've been so kind."

"Well, I best be getting back to the bunkhouse. We got plenty to do in the morning."

Chapter 24

Jim spent that night in a cold camp brooding over his decision. Cold camps were nothing new to him, but the aching in his gut was. Sleep didn't find him, and he broke camp before the sun was up. He had promised Elizabeth he would not go far, and he would keep his word, but he had no idea what he would do until his conscience would permit him to leave. Throwing his saddle onto Buck's back and tightening the cinch, he decided to ride into town. Perhaps he could find an excuse to stay around if he looked there. While he could just ride the countryside, he thought it best if he had a legitimate reason for staying in the area.

Arriving in town just after sunrise, he swung the horse to the rail in front of Aunt Mable's. Dismounting, he trudged through the door. Shoulders down, he meandered into the dining area to have a cup of coffee.

"What are you doing here and not out working? You look like you just got kicked by a mule."

"Thanks. I was hoping I looked better than I feel." Jim attempted a grin.

"What's wrong, child?" Aunt Mable inquired.

"Nothing that a good fight won't fix," he growled.

"Well I never thought I'd hear you hunting a fight. She must've gotten under your skin more than I thought." Aunt Mable puckered her brow as if in deep thought.

"What are you talking about? Who got under my skin?"

"Don't play coy with me. I'm too old to waste time with that. You know doggone good and well *who*. Now the question is, what're you going to do about it? You aren't going to run out on her, are you?"

Jim twisted uncomfortably under the questioning. "I'm no good for her, but I promised her I'd stay until the rustling was stopped. After that, I have to leave."

"You mean there is something that you are scared of after all?" Her knowing eyes twinkled slightly. "And how does she feel?"

"I don't know! What difference does that make? You know what I am. You've been out here long enough to recognize the kind of man I am, and she doesn't need that kind of man."

"Oh fiddlesticks! And yes, I do know what kind of man you are, and were, Mr. James Harding. You're just on uncertain ground and scared to death."

"Why does everyone keep telling me how scared I am? You, Whitey, her. I know what I'm doing."

Aunt Mable wisely changed the subject. "Well what are you going to do now? You can't just loaf and hope the rustlers go away, so what is your plan?"

"I don't know. I just knew I couldn't stay at the ranch any longer."

"Well the town could use a marshal. Maybe that would give you your excuse to stick around and a bit of officiality for hunting rustlers. I'll ask for you if you want."

"Sure." The suggestion seemed to fit in with his plans and might just provide him the means to accomplish what he had to do.

"I'm pretty sure that the folks here in town will be glad to have you on as marshal. There's been a rougher element showing up lately. It might mean fewer fights, and not too many will argue with your authority more than once. I'll head out right after breakfast if you want? Now you sit down, and I'll feed you with the rest of my guests."

"Thank you." Jim brightened slightly as he gained a little bit of direction. "I guess I could eat, and if you have a room, I wouldn't mind taking it for now."

Jim ate quickly and was given a room, as Aunt Mable put it: "For as long as you need it and pay your room and board." It seemed like just a few days had passed since he had ridden into town, but so much had happened. None of it was what he had planned. All he wanted was a meal and a place to sleep when he rode up to the hitching rail in front of Mickey's. How did things get so complicated?

After breakfast the next morning, Aunt Mable was ready to head out and start talking to the town leaders about her thoughts for a town marshal.

"We don't like punchers getting too rowdy while in town but don't have the money to pay someone either," was the sentiment they heard at each of the places they stopped.

"I guess I could work for the same wages Miss Davis was paying me." Jim smiled slightly.

"'Miss Davis!' You know her name as well as I do. What's your problem, boy? You called her Elizabeth before."

Jim's face clouded. "I don't want to talk about it. It's better this way is all."

"You're lucky I don't get the rolling pin out and knock some sense into you, but the town needs a marshal in good health. Besides, you'll talk about it when you're ready. Maybe they would take you on if you were working for free."

Jim stood silently for a few seconds before responding. Sparks danced in his blue eyes like so much lightning during a thunderstorm, but he held his tongue. He knew Aunt Mable meant well and could see right through him. Preacher had taught him: "When you're going to lose the argument anyway, it's better to not argue." He heeded that advice now.

"Okay. Let's present it this way. I'll do the job for whatever is offered. We can always say I'll supplement my salary with bounties on any wanted outlaw I apprehend."

"I think they just might do that. The town council has a meeting tomorrow night. Why not ask them then? The worst they could do is tell you no." Aunt Mable's idea was sound, and they decided to present it to the town council the next night. The rest of the day was uneventful.

When the time finally arrived for the village council to meet, Jim had spoken to all the members and was aware of what their decision would be, barring any unforeseen circumstances. Even so, he paced to and fro, waiting for his turn to present his suggestion. There was very little other business to tend to, but it seemed like hours before Jim was allowed to speak.

"Gentlemen, I'm not much of a speech-maker, so I'll make this brief," he began. "I know that there have been some minor problems here in town and in the area with, shall we say, 'rowdy' behavior. I know the town could use someone to help keep the peace, and I'd like to offer my help in that capacity, if I may. I'm willing to do the job for whatever the town council is willing and able to pay, and I can supplement my income with bounties from any wanted criminals I apprehend. If you can work with that, I'd like the job. I'll also be working on the rustling problem that's growing here. Well, that's it in a nutshell."

Jeremiah Thompson, the owner of the hardware store and the chairman of the council spoke up. "We can't afford much, but I think I speak for all of us when I say we'd like to have someone as capable as yourself as the marshal. We'll talk wages and let you know before we adjourn tonight. Give us a couple minutes to talk it over."

A few minutes later, the council offered Jim twenty-five dollars a month, and he became the new town marshal. The next day the blacksmith, a huge, quiet man, made a star and stamped the word *marshal* onto it for Jim. The newly appointed marshal was also given a vacant building to use as the temporary marshal's office and jail. It was a solidly built structure, and he affixed some rudimentary locks on the two doors of the now converted storage rooms. While nowhere near as secure as a proper jail, it would suffice for now. If he had to incarcerate someone truly dangerous, he knew of other ways of doing that. For now, he had his office. He had no idea how soon he would be making use of it nor what would happen there to change the tide of his life.

The next few days were spent wandering the town to find the most likely places for trouble to start and routes along which he could move quickly and surreptitiously from one end of town to the other. His father had taught him that arriving on the scene in time was good, but it was better to arrive in time and from a direction of your choosing.

Whitey stopped in to visit during a trip to town to get supplies. "We been being watched the last day or so, ever since your boys took that herd north. I hope they got through. Miss 'Lizabeth has been a fretting something fierce about you taking off. She don't think it shows none, but I got eyes what can see plain as day. I think them rustlers is planning to make a big grab. Probably won't be particular if they have to shoot their way out or not. Just my gut instinct, but it usually comes close to the mark."

"Have you talked to Thad about it? He could maybe send a few hands over to help. I'll ride out that way in the next few days and take a look around too. Maybe we can wrap this whole thing up within a couple weeks."

"Then what? You heading back up north? Not my never mind but you got something to think about right here once the smoke clears. It ain't so easy to ride off when you got yourself hobbled with thoughts of home and a woman what cares about you."

"Stop that foolish talk. You know who and what I am."

"Yes I do know, and I know a whole heap more than I did before you got here. You're running scared of the one thing you don't know nothing about. Like I said, it ain't my never mind, but it's something you should maybe think on before you toss it aside. Now as for talking to Thad, I done did that already. He says he's had that feeling too of being watched. He'll be ready, I think. I better get them supplies and head back to the ranch. Come on out and say 'howdy' sometime."

"Maybe I will do that. I haven't really had a chance to catch up on what's going on up at the home ranch, and I'm sure Skipper could fill me in plus half of what took place in the next three territories."

"You do that, and I'll even clean the coffeepot for you." The oldster snickered as he left the marshal's office.

Chapter 25

That night, while making his rounds, Jim noticed several strangers lounging around town. None were doing anything to attract attention, but that itself seemed odd to Jim. The warning bells in his head were ringing loud and clear, but he could do nothing if they behaved themselves, and all of them pulled out just before midnight. He wandered the town that night watching for anything out of place or for any disturbance, but all was quiet. Even so, the hairs on the back of his neck stood on end the whole night. Just before daybreak, Jim returned to Aunt Mable's to try and get a little bit of sleep.

"I can't put my finger on it, Aunt Mable, but something is in the air. Whitey said he felt like they were being watched out at the ranch, and last night the town had half a dozen strangers in it. I think I'll take a ride out to the S Bar S later today and have a talk with Whitey and the boys. Maybe they can shed some light on it. I don't like it."

Aunt Mable smiled before replying, "Maybe you should talk to someone else while you're out that way. She told me last time we spoke she doesn't know why you left. Don't you think she deserves an explanation at least?"

"Arrgh! Why do I even try? Okay, I'll talk to her. I can't seem to get a minute of peace without you or somebody else telling me how foolish I'm being. Can I talk to you seriously for a few minutes?"

"Of course you can. I'm all ears, and I can keep my trap shut if it's private. It's about Beth Ann, isn't it?"

"As a matter of fact, it is. I think by now you've figured out who I am."

"I'm not so naïve that I couldn't figure that out. I've heard your name before. Many a time."

"Then you know why I can't stay and why she's better off without me, don't you? I mean, I was a killer. I hunted men with the intention of killing them, and I did it. There's blood on my hands, and I can't expect her to overlook that, can I?"

"Dearie, you're not that man anymore. Fact being, you never was. You just lost your way. She knows you better than you think, and she already made up her mind what kind of man you are. Don't run out on her without talking to her. You're a better man than that."

Jim screwed his face in thought before responding. "Can you do me a favor?" he inquired. "I have something that I've carried around with me for quite a while. If something happens to me, could you give this to Elizabeth for me?" Jim produced a small wooden box carefully wrapped in parchment paper. "Hold it for me, but if something happens, give it to Elizabeth. She's the only one I have ever met that my mother would want to have it."

As he placed the box in her hand, she swallowed. "I'll hold it for you, but what is it? Why don't you give it to her?"

"You and I both know what I'm riding into. I can't tell you what it is, but will you do as I asked?"

"Of course I will, but you better come back and give it to her yourself, or I'll give you the business." Aunt Mable knew full well that more than one marshal had returned over their saddle when chasing rustlers. Jim was a good man; but he was a man nonetheless, and bullets didn't discriminate. Good men could die too. A tear slipped down her cheek as she hugged Jim. "Now you get on out of here and go find those rustlers. And then you marry that girl."

"The rustlers I know how to deal with. As for the other…" Jim left it at that and walked to the stable to saddle Buck. Swinging astride, he pointed the horse north toward he knew not what for sure. Changing his mind on his way out of town, he headed instead for the Swinging M.

Jim rode into mass confusion as he approached the ranch house. Riders from the C&O and D/C faced off against the few riders on the grounds of the Swinging M. Thad Morrish stood next to Dean and presented a formidable presence, but his riders were too few and already stood under the guns of the other ranches.

Riding in at a lope, Jim interrupted whatever was taking place. Placing himself between the two factions, he turned to David Cochran. "What's all this about, Dave?"

"The C&O rode into our place this morning. It seems they lost a huge bunch of cattle last night, and the night guard was found dead. We lost several hundred head too and had a couple of our punchers shot up pretty bad. Surprised you didn't run into our men going in to get the doc.

Well, we followed the herds across some of the trails east of here heading northwest. Thad didn't take too kindly to us crossing his range without his consent. I guess we had a few questions as to why, especially when we found some of our stock scattered across his range mixed in with some of his stock. The last few nights, some of my boys saw his foreman riding the back trails. On the way here, we found him with some of the stolen cattle and a bullet in his back. Maybe one of the guys that got bushwhacked got in a lucky shot. Guess we'll never know, but it looked like Thad might be up to something dirty to us."

"Frank Baxter never stole a cow in his life!" Jim responded hotly before Thad could speak. "Think about it, man. If a rustler was pushing cattle at night, and quickly, they'd lose a few head and those would gather with any local cows. Maybe Frank came up on the rustlers and got the same treatment your boys got. Did you think about that? And who wouldn't be upset with someone riding into their yard first thing in the morning and throwing around accusations and making demands?"

He could still read distrust in the faces of the mounted men. Swiveling in the saddle, he spoke to the owner of the Swinging M. "Thad, why don't you send some of your riders with these men to hunt down the herd? You and Dean ride with me, and we'll send the riders from the S Bar S to catch up. We can ride into town and let these men sort it out."

Thad gave instructions to his riders, and he and Dean quickly saddled up and rode with Jim to the S Bar S. They found Dwayne riding into the ranch yard with news of the rustlers hitting the herd.

"Jim, there must have been about twenty or thirty riders. They were pushing critters with everybody's brand. Must've had five or six hundred head. Whitey and the others are following the herd. He sent me back to get some help. Skipper got nicked, but he insisted he'll get his payback."

"There's already help on the way. Thad and Dean are going to ride into town with me to sort things out. It seems there were some wrong conclusions jumped to earlier. You better ride back out and warn the boys about the other ranchers coming their way. We don't want any more wrong ideas floating around. We need to focus on the rustlers not blaming each other."

As Dwayne turned back in the direction he had just ridden in from, Jim swung down in front of the house. "I need to speak with Miss Davis. I don't think she should be out here by herself with what's going on. It isn't safe for her."

Thad laughed. "You go right ahead. She's probably more dangerous than any rustlers anyway."

Jim's face turned red, but he mounted the steps and knocked.

The door swung open. "Oh, Jim. It's you. I thought I heard Dwayne talking to someone. Where is he? What are Dean and Thad doing here? And why are you here?"

"I sent Dwayne back out to join Whitey and the rest of the men. We had some problems with rustlers last night. Thad and Dean are riding into town with me. I don't think it's safe for you to stay out here alone right now. If one of those men should stop by and find you alone..." Jim didn't finish the comment, but the implication was quite clear. Thad and Dean nodded their agreement.

"He's right, Miss Davis. Begging your pardon, but you are a right pretty woman, and those men are not ones to trust under any circumstances. You being alone out here would make me feel awfully nervous until I knew you was safe."

"Why thank you, Thad. That is very kind of you. Can you wait a few minutes for me, and I'll ride into town with you? I'm sure Aunt Mable will want to hear what is going on too. She worries over Whitey sometimes."

She reemerged from the house a few minutes later. Jim had hitched up the buggy and helped her into the driver's seat. "I think we have something to talk about too, but that might have to wait. I'll explain it later. For now let's get you into town where you'll be safe. You can stay with Aunt Mable until this gets cleared up."

Elizabeth controlled her curiosity about whatever it was that Jim said they needed to talk about but couldn't keep from asking about the rustling. "Did they hit everybody? When did it happen? Why are you going to town instead of after them?"

"Whoa, one question at a time. First, yes, they did hit every ranch last night. That's what caused the confusion. Some of the other riders thought that since the herd passed across Thad's place and Frank was found dead near some of the stolen cattle, then Thad and Dean were involved."

"Frank Baxter was killed? He was such a gentleman. I am so sorry, Thad."

"Umm, thank you," Thad muttered. "He was a good man."

The rest of the ride to town was quiet, but the town was bustling upon their arrival. Several people stared as the quartet rode down the main street toward Aunt Mable's. It seemed that the riders who had come in to find the doctor had done a bit of talking, and a rumor had begun to spread. It seemed that the words of Psalms 52:2 were proving true once again: "The tongue deviseth mischiefs; like a sharp razor, working deceitfully" (KJV). Jim began to wonder if he had made the right choice by asking Thad and Dean to come to town rather than ride with those hunting the rustlers.

"Why ain't they in chains?" the owner of the local hardware demanded. "We pay you to lock up crooks, not ride to town with them."

Jim swiveled toward the speaker. His face hardened, and his eyes clouded like a tempest on a cold sea. "I only chain prisoners, Thompson," he growled. "Thad and Dean are my guests. If you have something to say about it, then come over to my office, and we'll discuss it there, not out here on the street."

Thompson tried to stare the marshal down but failed miserably and turned away, muttering under his breath.

"It seems we aren't so welcome here right now, Marshal. I hope our men are doing better out there on the range convincing the other ranchers they're not guilty of anything. Probably better for them if we're not along though. I'd likely blow my stack and cause more trouble. I'm not always the most patient of men, if you hadn't noticed that as yet."

"Rumors and innuendo will get you in trouble faster than the truth every time. I just hope that folks think before they speak or act. Until the crews get back, we're kinda stuck. It might be best if we holed up at the jail until then. The walls are solid, and I can hopefully talk sense to anyone who tries to start trouble."

Dean spoke up, "What do you mean 'start trouble'? We didn't do nothing wrong. Why would there be trouble?"

"Some men just want to think the worst of those they are jealous of or who have more than they do. I guess it's human nature. They try to rationalize it as fairness, but it's just thinking the worst of others—probably why one of the Ten Commandments is not to covet. God knows us better than we know ourselves."

The small party stopped in front of Aunt Mable's. Jim dismounted and helped Elizabeth from the buggy. "I'll be right back out. I just want to fill Aunt Mable in on what's going on. Keep a sharp eye out."

"You go on. The lapdogs in this town will steer clear of us for now. Take your time." Thad smiled confidently at Jim and waved him off to the house.

Aunt Mable was found in the parlor enjoying a cup of coffee and some leftover Danish. "Why aren't you out catching those rustlers? Or did you catch them already?"

"According to some people here in town, I have, but it isn't Thad and Dean like they think. They just rode in with me because of some hard feelings out there. Why do folks have to go off half cocked? If they just wait for all the facts, they would save a lot of people a lot of trouble."

"The Swinging M rustlers? Pish posh. Thad and Dean might be obnoxious and belligerent, but they ain't rustlers. Who would even think such a thing?"

"It seems that some of the riders from the D/C found Frank's body with some of the stolen cattle and added two and two and came up with seventeen. I just hope the folks here in town keep their heads and don't act foolish. We'll be over at the jail waiting for the ranch crews to return."

"You didn't let that old goat Whitey ride after them rustlers by himself, did you?" Aunt Mable asked anxiously.

"No. He has plenty of company. Could you keep an eye on Elizabeth until this is over?"

"I don't need someone to watch out for me! I'm a grown woman and can watch out for myself. Just who do you think you're talking to or about?"

"Why, Miss Davis, I am talking to one of the wisest ladies in these parts about one of the loveliest ladies in these parts. And yes, indeed, you are a grown woman. Please stay here, if for no other reason than to keep Aunt Mable company. Would you do that for me please?"

"Fine. But only to keep Aunt Mable happy and not for you."

"Thank you. I'd better get going. Thad and Dean are waiting out front."

Jim turned and retraced his steps out the front door of the boardinghouse.

Elizabeth stomped her foot. "Ugh! Can you believe the nerve of that man? Thinking I need someone to look after me. Why, I was doing just fine before he came along." Her face was crimson with anger, and she clenched and unclenched her small fists. "Why I have half a mind to—"

"To what, dearie? He just wants to make sure you're safe is all. Maybe he's a bit overprotective, but he means well. Give him a little bit of an opportunity, and you'd find him a real gem. Of course all gems need some polishing. That's where us womenfolk come in." Aunt Mable smiled at the young woman pacing the floor in front of her. "Now come sit here before you wear a hole in my rug."

The three men rode the rest of the way to the new marshal's office and dismounted. They walked inside and settled in to wait. Something was brewing, and all three could sense it. Jim prayed that it would hold off until Whitey returned with the real rustlers in tow, dead, or driven from the country. Time was against the men in the jail.

Later that afternoon, Aunt Mable brought the men some sandwiches to eat. "I figured you'd be hungry since you probably haven't eaten all day. Eat up."

"Why thank you, Miss Mable." Thad's response was warm and friendly. "I reckon we ruffled a few feathers here in town with the way I let my crew and my boy act. Sure is good to see at least one friendly face. Maybe I'll have to tame things down a bit from now on."

"You're more than welcome, Thad, but you're right that you do need to tighten them reins up some. Most don't remember when you and Millie first got here, but I do. She wouldn't have liked you being so roughshod."

"You knew my ma?"

"Oh, my child, I know everybody here abouts."

"You're right, Miss Mable. Guess it's coming back to bite me now. Dean, you pay attention to what Miss Mable has to say. She is a knowing woman."

Dean looked baffled at the respect his father showed to this old woman. Since his mother's death, he had never heard his father offer this much deference to anyone. "Um, sure, Pa."

"As for you, Marshal, you might want to take a walk around town before dark. Things are too quiet, if you know what I mean. And there's plenty being served over at The Rusty Nail."

"I'll do that right now. Thad and Dean, you better hole up here and wait for me. Aunt Mable, I'll walk you back home now, if you don't mind."

"That sounds like a good idea. Shall we?"

Jim took Aunt Mable by the arm, and the two walked back to the boardinghouse before Jim went about his duty. "She won't say it, but she sure is mad you're leaving the country. Why, she darn near wore a hole in my floor pacing around all worried-like today. Don't you ride out without talking to her. That just wouldn't be right."

200

"I can't think on that right now. There's something more pressing to deal with right now. I'll talk to both of you later, if I'm able." Jim's somber tone made Aunt Mable look closely at the young man beside her.

"You do what needs done. We'll be waiting."

Jim smiled slightly. "Thanks."

Walking to The Rusty Nail, Jim thought hard about what he needed to do. If he could head things off, he would do so. If not, he would stand his ground and let the chips fall where they may.

Standing outside the bar, Jim closed one eye and counted a slow count to fifty before stepping into the interior of the bar. By doing so, his eyes adjusted much more quickly to the dimly lit barroom, something both his father and Preacher had taught him to do.

The bar had more patrons than was usual for the time of day and was unusually quiet for so many customers. That was a bad sign. What little conversation there had been before Jim walked in ceased when he was recognized.

"Why don't you men head for home? I'm sure your families would like to see you."

"Why aren't they in chains, Marshal? They found some of the cows on their spread."

"Wait until all the ranch crews get back. Then we can sort the truth out. Right now all you have is rumor and half the story. Now go on home and sleep it off."

"We ain't breaking no laws, Marshal."

"True enough but remember what I said."

Jim returned to the jail and barred the door. "It didn't go so well. If they come this way, you better let me do the talking, and stay out of sight. I'll keep the shotgun loaded just in case."

Thad's brow furrowed. "Is it really that bad?"

"I'm not sure, Thad, but it sure didn't look friendly out there. What puncher got killed, and what one's got shot up? If they were well liked, that would explain the desire for revenge."

"I'm not sure, but I didn't see Conway with them that rode into the ranch yard. Maybe he was one that got shot some."

"No matter. We'll just hold out here until the ranch crews get back."

"Why not just ride out?" Dean asked.

"It'd look like we was running, and they'd figure us guilty for sure. Ain't that right, Jim?"

"You got it right, Thad. We'll just sit tight and ride the storm out."

With the doors barred and the lamps dimmed, the three men drifted off to sleep.

Chapter 26

A pair of riders stepped down in front of the saloon and walked inside. The somber mood and large crowd gave rise to an idea for the smiling blond. "Why so quiet tonight? It looks like a wake in here."

"There was a raid on the herds in the valley, and some of the boys got shot up some. One of them was killed," one of the townsfolk responded.

"Yeah, and the marshal has two of them that we think was responsible over to the jail right now, but he says they're innocent."

"He does, does he? What makes him so sure of that?"

"It's just his say-so. Since he started marshaling instead of ramrodding the S Bar S, he thinks he is the law." The booze was distorting the minds of otherwise sensible men.

The blond stranger knew instantly who the new marshal was and how he might exact his revenge. Only a short time before, he and Keegan had slipped away from the rest of the gang just as the ranch crews were closing in. The fight would last a long time, but in the end he knew that the rustlers were done for. He thought that while the battle was being waged miles away, he could escape with the proceeds from their earlier endeavors and possibly pick up a bit more on his way out of the country. Keegan could prove useful, so he brought him along.

Seeing a means to take vengeance, Smiling Bob set about stirring the pot with well-placed hints that a rope was what the rustlers deserved and that the marshal needed to step out of the way, or maybe he should be locked up or hung himself. As the crowd grew more and more vocal about lynching the Morrishes, he pulled Keegan aside.

"When we get them down by the jail and that marshal steps out, you plug him good. Nobody will be able to say where the shot came from, and they're ready for a lynching anyway, so they won't even give it a thought."

Keegan smiled. This would put an end to the nightmares he had been having since seeing Jim alive after all of the years had passed. "Sure thing, boss."

Smiling Bob fed the blood lust of the crowd until at last he had his lynch mob ready to go. He urged them out into the street and on toward the makeshift jail on the edge of town.

Jim awoke with a start. They were coming.

"Stay inside. I'll do my best to break it up. They know I won't back down, so I'm hopeful they will. I'll take the ten gauge in case they decide they don't want to go home. Nobody likes to face one of those things."

Jim stepped out onto the porch. He could hear them clomping in his direction. "Lord, I don't want to have to shoot anybody. Give me the discernment to know who to single out and what words to use."

Jim stood before the door of the marshal's office. The twin barrels of the 10-gauge express gun rested negligently in the crook of his left arm, and his right hand gripped the stock just behind the double set of triggers. The shiny star symbolizing his office was pinned above the left breast pocket of his faded blue shirt. Torchlight from the mob glittered against the silver star, making it look like a tiny light in an otherwise dark night.

These were people he had come to know and care about, but his duty and oath to uphold the law held him firmly where he was. Unwavering in the face of the crowd, he was a very lonely figure. He'd known lawmen to die in this same situation standing against good people perpetrating an evil act. He'd seen others give in to the crowd as Pontius Pilate had done with Jesus almost nineteen hundred years before. There were still others who had prevailed without firing a shot, and some had been forced to kill to stand against a lynch mob.

"That's far enough!" His voice rang out loud and clear. "You know me, and you know that the only way to take these men is through me. They are not my prisoners, but they are under my protection. Are you willing to become murderers just to lynch two innocent men? Are you ready to face your wives and children and say, 'I was part of that mob that lynched Dean and Thad Morrish'? Are you?"

"They're guilty as sin!" came a shout from the back of the crowd. Several other voices echoed the sentiment, and the crowd began to surge forward. "Step aside, Marshal, or we'll come right over you!"

Other voices could be heard. "They found those D/C cows on his spread!" "Baxter was found right there with the stolen cattle!" Others joined in the cacophony as the crowd started forward again.

The ten gauge swiveled from the crook of Jim's arm to point in the general direction of the crowd. "I said that's far enough! Go home and think about what you're doing. I don't want to hurt anyone, but I will give the doctor some business if I have to."

The crowd stopped and began to waver. Jim hoped and prayed that they would disperse. He had meant what he had said.

The same voice from the back of the crowd shouted again. "He won't shoot. Rush him!" The voice was familiar, but he couldn't place it yet. If he could just find the speaker, he could end the situation by calling him out, but he had secreted himself in the back of the crowd and was indistinguishable. Jim could feel their hesitation and started to press his advantage when the shot rang out.

Jim's hat was torn from his head, and a deep furrow was cut along the side of his skull. Lights exploded in his brain, and then darkness enveloped him as he collapsed onto the boardwalk. He was unaware of the voice in the back of the crowd urging them forward or of the keys to the jail being taken from his belt.

He awoke a few minutes later to the sobbing of Elizabeth as she wiped the blood from his face. He could hear the lynch mob near the oak tree in the center of town as they pushed forward with their evil plans. The last time he had been struck unconscious by a bullet, he had been unable to recover in time to keep murder from being done. This time he had to try.

Gently pushing Elizabeth from him, he struggled to find his feet and his equilibrium. Even now he might be too late, but he had to try. It was his duty, and he was honor bound to do it.

"Don't go. They'll kill you. Please," Elizabeth pleaded.

"I have to," was Jim's reply.

Aunt Mable had found her way to the jail and gently pulled Elizabeth's arms from Jim as he started to stagger down the street.

"Jim, please" Elizabeth sobbed as he moved toward the crowd, bloody and hatless. His macabre weaving gate moved him away from her, and she turned to Aunt Mable. "Why? They'll kill him and still lynch the Morrishes. Why does he have to go?"

Aunt Mable took Elizabeth's hands gently in hers. "He has it to do, child. You wouldn't want him if he didn't go. You might not believe it now, but you would have come to think of him as a coward if he hadn't gone. He wouldn't be the man for you either if he let you talk him into breaking his word to uphold the law."

"But they'll kill him."

"Maybe, child, but he has it to do. He's a good man." She smiled at her young friend. "You love him, don't you?"

As Elizabeth nodded tearfully, gunfire erupted in the middle of Lone Oak. The deep bellow of the heavy ten gauge was followed closely by several sharp barks of pistol shots. Aunt Mable caught Elizabeth as she started to run toward the sound. "You wait here," she ordered. "You can't stop it, and you'll only distract him from what he has to do. We'll both go when the shooting stops."

Chapter 27

Stumbling in the direction of the town square, Jim was unaware of the scene he was leaving behind. He was barely aware of picking up the shotgun before heading toward what he saw as his duty. Instinctively he checked the loads while walking and loosened his pistols in their holsters. He would stop the lynching if possible. If not, he would arrest the leaders of the lynch mob. Friends or not, they were not above the law.

He slowed his shuffling gate as he came to the edge of the square. Leaning against the hardware store, Jim wiped away the blood that had flowed into his eyes and shook his head to clear the cobwebs from his ringing brain. Blood droplets flicked from his wound to sprinkle against the store wall. A quick survey of the situation showed him that instant action was needed.

The mob had dragged their captives to the base of the oak tree and was fixing a noose around the neck of each of them. The younger Morrish showed the terror that he was feeling as his hands were yanked behind his back to be tied.

He managed to break free for a brief moment and tried to run, but the man holding the noose pulled him backward onto the ground. The crowd quickly overpowered him and bound his hands.

Thad Morrish stood his ground and called the mob for the cowards he saw them to be. His only plea was for his son. "Get off him! Leave him be! I'm the one you want. You're nothing but a pack of yellow curs." He hurled other insults at the crowd.

As they dragged Dean closer to the tree, Thad charged into the cluster in defense of his son. Barreling men over like so many empty bottles, he used his size and strength to come to his son's aid. Had his hands not been tied, he surely would have been successful. Even so, he delivered powerful kicks to those holding Dean. Using his heavy shoulders, he shoved others aside like chafe before a strong wind. Just as he reached his son, the noose around his neck was jerked tight, and he was dragged from his son's side.

The end of the rope around his neck was dallied to the saddle horn of the horse of one his captors and was already running over a stout limb in the huge oak tree. When the spurs were put to his mount, the horse leaped forward at the unexpected treatment.

Thad would never know if he had been successful or not in his endeavor to save his son. The rope around his neck was jerked so violently that his powerful neck was snapped like a dry twig. He was dead instantly, and his body was dragged up to hang from the limb. The nerves in his legs had not yet received the message from his brain that the powerful frame they had once carried was now a lifeless shell. They kicked spasmodically while Thad's body dangled at the end of the cruel rope.

From the shadows near the corner of the hardware an eerie figure emerged. Shotgun in hand, Jim rushed into the torch lit square. Too late to save Thad from being hanged, he still sought to try. Dropping to a knee, he swung the heavy express gun to his shoulder and squeezed both triggers. The loads from both barrels found their mark, and the horse holding Thad in the air crashed lifeless to the ground. The rider tumbled to the dirt, but the rope remained wrapped fast around the saddle horn, and Thad continued his ghoulish "death dance" several feet above the ground.

One of the men holding Dean went for his gun as soon as the shotgun belched. Knowing he wouldn't have time to reload, Jim threw the empty express to the side and drew as he rose to his feet. Both six-guns were in his hands when a bullet struck him along the ribs. The shooter was the smiling blond drifter who had helped to stir up the crowd for the lynching.

Jim took careful aim to make sure he didn't hit anyone but his intended target. Smiling Bob jerked violently as if slugged by an invisible fist. He stared disbelievingly from Jim to the blood soaking his shirtfront before his knees buckled, and he crumpled into the dust, still smiling. Murder and theft had been his way of life and had now led him to this inglorious death. Boot Hill and Lucifer both had special places for such men.

The rest of the crowd scattered like chickens before a hawk as the marshal came toward them. His scalp wound leaked blood down his face, and the wound in his upper body oozed blood onto the side of his shirt. One terrified man remained frozen in place. His face drained of all color. Before he could force himself to flee, Jim slammed him to the ground with the butt of the heavy pistol in his right hand. Dean was left alone with the bloody marshal.

Sliding his knife from its sheath, Jim cut the bonds holding Dean's wrists together and took the noose from around his neck. He gently slipped the razor-sharp knife into Dean's hands. "Go cut your father down. He deserves better than that."

Jim followed as Dean moved mechanically toward the gently twisting body of his father. The still form of the rider who had snatched the life from Thad began to stir. Pushing himself to his feet, he turned to see both Dean and Jim walking in his direction.

"No! I shot you!" Panic and terror filled his eyes as he grabbed for the gun on his hip. "You're supposed to be dead!" he screamed.

Twelve years had aged him, but there was no mistaking the thin face, Roman nose, and bug-eyed look of the last living attacker of the Lazy H Ranch. He had stopped hunting for him years before, assuming him to be dead or far out of the country, but there he stood. Keegan was the name that had long been forgotten. Recognition slowed Jim's reaction only slightly.

"You're dead! I killed you!" Screeching unintelligible, terror-filled words, Keegan began blasting away. His bullets kicked up dirt geysers and slammed into buildings several feet off target. In his terror, he could not align his gun on his intended target.

Jim stepped toward him, carefully firing each time his foot struck the ground. At ten paces, he stopped and finished emptying his revolvers into the convulsing body of a man who had tried to kill him on multiple occasions, including this very night. Keegan, who had helped to butcher his family more than ten years before, was dead before he hit the ground, and the last haunting memory of that terrible day was swept from Jim's mind. He walked to the body and looked down at his fallen foe.

As the last echoes of gunfire died away, a tearful Elizabeth rushed from beside the hardware store to throw her arms around Jim. Taking her by the shoulders, he untangled himself from her arms.

"I've one last thing to do, and then I have a question for you. First, I need you to go get Thompson and tell him I need an axe. Will you do that for me?"

Elizabeth nodded and set off to do as Jim had asked.

Both of Jim's wounds had all but stopped bleeding. The bullet that had struck him in the ribs had only grazed his ribcage, glancing off one of the strong bones. His constant exercise and hard work helped him to shrug off the effects to some extent. Helping Dean lower his father's body to the ground, he took the noose from around the big man's neck.

"I know we didn't always get along on the best of terms," Jim spoke softly, "but I think your father did what he thought was right. I think he was a good man. I'm very sorry. Take him home."

"He wasn't always a hard man. After my mother died, he kinda always tried to be strong. It made him harder than he wanted to be. I think he blamed hisself for bringing her here."

"Take him home and bury him by your mother's side. I think that they would both want that."

A contrite Thompson arrived then with a sharp, heavy new axe. He had been in the mob and knew what they had done was wrong. He handed the axe to Jim, who tested the edge with his thumb. Finding the blade plenty sharp, he turned and gave Thompson a command.

"Get a buckboard and take Thaddeus Morrish home. Take part of your mob with you and dig him a decent grave. Dean will show you where. We'll have his funeral whenever Dean says, and the town *will* be there to pay their respects. Am I clear?"

"Yes, sir, Mr. Harding," was the subdued response.

As soon as Thad's body was on the way to the Swinging M, Jim ordered everyone from the town square. The S Bar S crew had arrived with reinforcements from the Swinging M and stood ready to enforce his orders if need be.

Only Whitey dared to approach Jim during the night. He passed some information to Jim that might have saved Thad, had it been received just twenty minutes earlier. "We caught up with the rustlers afore they got through the pass. They decided to fight. That Smiling Bob feller and one other was already gone when we arrived. I see they didn't get too far. Sorry we didn't get back sooner." Jim simply nodded at the news and threw himself even deeper into his labor.

Throughout the night the ring of an axe striking wood could be heard. It didn't stop until about an hour before dawn when the groaning of a great tree preceded its crash to the ground.

Elizabeth watched as Jim pushed himself through the night. Like some automaton, he continued to swing the axe, sending huge chips flying from the trunk of the giant oak. Aunt Mable stood by her side in the cool night air.

"I know. He's got it to do," a tearful Elizabeth whispered to her friend.

As soon as the tree crashed to the ground, Elizabeth and Aunt Mable walked to Jim's side. He wiped the sweat from his brow and leaned heavily on the axe. "The lynching tree won't ever be used for a lynching party again." He panted.

Exhausted, Jim sank the blade of the axe into the stump and allowed himself to be led to the boardwalk where he slumped to the rough boards. His hands, though long used to hard work, were blistered and bleeding. His shoulders ached from the nonstop swinging of the axe, and his head throbbed like the beating of Cheyenne war drums. The bullet that had struck him in the ribs had glanced off one of them and left a nasty gash that looked far worse than it actually was. Even so, it had started to seep blood again.

Elizabeth tenderly took his hands in hers and opened them. She tore part of her petticoat and dipped it into the nearby rain barrel before gently washing the blood from his hands. By the time Aunt Mable returned with Dr. Halloran, she had repeated this process for each of his wounds, gently washing the dirt, sweat, and dried blood from each of them. Under her ministrations, exhaustion took over, and Jim faded off to sleep.

The doctor and Aunt Mable found them still on the boardwalk. Elizabeth had laid Jim's head in her lap and had drifted to sleep herself with her hand holding a damp cloth on his scalp wound.

Aunt Mable smiled and whispered to Dr. Halloran, "I think he's in good hands."

The doctor chuckled softly in agreement. "I still think I should check him over," he whispered, "but I hate to interrupt his rest. He needs it right now."

"I'll do it for you." Aunt Mable smiled. "I think he'll rest better in a bed than on the boardwalk. Besides, this may just be a ruse to get out of asking someone a question."

The doctor cocked a quizzical eye but said nothing. Aunt Mable just giggled and touched Elizabeth softly on the shoulder.

Opening her eyes to see Aunt Mable's grinning face, Elizabeth awoke with a start. "I must have dozed off for a few minutes," she mumbled.

"That's all right, child," Aunt Mable said. "Your man needs some tending to, and the doctor's here now. Before the doctor starts working on him though, did he ask his question?"

Elizabeth gave Aunt Mable a puzzled look.

"He has you treatin' his wounds and fussin' and frettin' that he might get killed, and then he thinks, just because he's been shot a couple of times, he can get out it? I'll give him a few more lumps if that's what he thinks," the oldster fumed.

Jim had caught her mock threats and opened his left eye. He smiled up at Aunt Mable. "I guess I had better ask that question then if I don't want any more pain inflicted upon my poor, abused body." Thinking quickly, he continued. "Elizabeth, would you mind if we painted the bunkhouse green?"

As both women stared at him in bewilderment, he burst into fits of laughter, which baffled them all the more.

"I think that head wound might be more serious than it looks," Aunt Mable muttered. "If not, I might just give him one of my own."

Jim stopped laughing. "Aunt Mable, do you have that box I asked you to keep with you?"

Eyeing Jim suspiciously, she replied, "Of course I do. It's right here." She quickly produced the small, paper-wrapped box from the pocket of her dress.

With the doctor's help, Jim gained his feet. He tenderly took the box from Aunt Mable and stood before Elizabeth.

"Elizabeth," he started, "we've been through a lot together. Until recently, I was just a tumbleweed blowing from place to place. I've wanted a home and family, but I always felt that there was something left to do or something missing. I think I've finally found that which was missing. That something was someone. That someone is you. Elizabeth Angela Davis, will you make me a very happy man and consent to be my wife?"

A tearful Elizabeth threw herself into his arms, wrapping hers tightly around his neck. She nearly knocked them both to the ground as she planted a passion-filled kiss on his lips.

"You'd better say yes and save that stuff for the wedding night," the elder of the two witnesses teased with a smile and tears of her own.

"Yes, yes, yes!" Elizabeth exclaimed.

At that, Jim opened the small box for Elizabeth to see. Inside was a beautiful ring made of gold with a dark blue, almost black, sapphire set in it. "This is my pledge to you."

Chapter 28

The entire town showed up for Thad's funeral, and the preacher preached a beautiful message of love, transgression, and redemption.

A few weeks later, there was a double wedding, and the S Bar S lost its oldest puncher. Whitey McKay had succumbed to the charms of one Mable Louise Harris, better known as Aunt Mable. Apparently they had been more than friends for a long time.

With the influx of cattle and working capital, the S Bar S prospered, as did the whole area surrounding Lone Oak.

As the spring thaw began and the leaves returned to the trees, Elizabeth and Jim learned that there would be a new addition to the Harding family. The winter had been a gentle one, and all of the ranches had come through it in excellent shape. Dean Morrish married Olivia Olson, Oliver's oldest daughter, and the area had peace.

One other thing happened that spring. Where Jim had sank the axe into the stump, a sprig had sprouted up, a tender shoot that would someday itself become a huge lone oak.

> And there shall come forth a rod out of the stump of Jesse, and a Branch shall grow out of his roots: And the spirit of the LORD shall rest upon him, the spirit of wisdom and understanding, the spirit of counsel and might, the spirit of knowledge and of the fear of the LORD; And shall make him of quick understanding in the fear of the LORD: and he shall not judge after the sight of his eyes, neither reprove after the hearing of his ears: But with righteousness shall he judge the poor, and reprove with equity for the meek of the earth: and he shall smite the earth: with the rod of his mouth, and with the breath of his lips shall he slay the wicked.
>
> —Isa. 11:1–4, KJV